Mary Liu Kao, PhD, MLS, MS

Introduction to Technical Services for Library Technicians

The Haworth Information Press®
An Imprint of The Haworth Press, Inc.
New York • London • Oxford

Introduction to Technical Services for Library Technicians

HAWORTH Cataloging & Classification
Ruth C. Carter, Senior Editor

New, Recent, and Forthcoming Titles:

Technical Services: A Quarter Century of Change: A Look to the Future by Linda C. Smith and Ruth C. Carter

Cataloging and Classification for Library Technicians, Second Edition by Mary Liu Kao

Introduction to Technical Services for Library Technicians by Mary Liu Kao

Introduction to Technical Services for Library Technicians

Mary Liu Kao, PhD, MLS, MS

The Haworth Information Press®
An Imprint of The Haworth Press, Inc.
New York • London • Oxford

Published by

The Haworth Information Press®, an imprint of The Haworth Press, Inc., 10 Alice Street, Binghamton, NY 13904-1580.

Cover design by Jennifer M. Gaska.

Library of Congress Cataloging-in-Publication Data

Kao, Mary Liu.
    Introduction to technical services for library technicians / Mary Liu Kao.
       p. cm.
    Includes bibliographical references and index.
    ISBN 0-7890-1488-2 (alk. paper) — ISBN 0-7890-1489-0 (pbk. : alk. paper)
    1. Technical services (Libraries)—United States. 2. Library technicians—United States. I. Title.

Z688.6.U6 K36 2001
025'.02—dc21
                                                   00-069623

To my late parents,
Yen-Huai and R. Bardina Liu,
I miss you, forever.

To my children,
Patricia and Christopher,
I love you, forever.

ABOUT THE AUTHOR

Mary Liu Kao, PhD, MLS, MS, has worked as a circulation librarian, a reference librarian, and a technical services librarian, and was Director of Library Services and Coordinator of the Library Technology Program at Three Rivers Community Technical College, in Norwich, Connecticut, for more than twenty-five years. She began teaching cataloging and classification in 1974 and has conducted numerous workshops for librarians and library technicians. Her book *Cataloging and Classification for Library Technicians* was first published in 1995 and has recently been published again in a second edition by The Haworth Press, Inc. Dr. Kao is now a training consultant at Innovative Interfaces, Inc., in Emeryville, California.

CONTENTS

Preface   xi

Chapter 1. Introduction   1

Terminology   1
Library Organization   2
Library Technical Services   2
Library Personnel   4
Library Technicians   4
Library Technicians in Technical Services   8
Review Questions   8

Chapter 2. Computers in Technical Services   9

Terminology   9
Computers   10
Library Automation   13
Automation and Technical Services   15
Review Questions   17

Chapter 3. Bibliographic Utilities and Networks   19

Terminology   20
Bibliographic Utilities and Networks   21
Networks and Library Cooperation   24
Integrated Automation Systems   24
Databases   25
Review Questions   26

Chapter 4. Acquisitions   27

Terminology   27
Types of Materials Acquired   29
Collection Development   31
Publishers, Producers, and Vendors   32

Acquisitions Procedures   32
Gifts and Exchanges   37
Review Questions   38

Chapter 5. Cataloging and Classification   **39**

Terminology   39
The Catalog   42
Elements of a Bibliographic Record   43
Cataloging   44
The MARC Record   55
Cataloging and Processing Routines   56
Review Questions   57

Chapter 6. Government Publications   **59**

Terminology   59
The Government Printing Office   60
Superintendent of Documents Classification System   64
Maintenance of Government Publications   68
Review Questions   69

Chapter 7. Serials   **71**

Terminology   72
Ordering   74
Cataloging   75
Serials Control   77
E-Journals   84
Review Questions   85

Chapter 8. Preservation   **87**

Terminology   87
Preservation and Conservation   88
The Problem of Deterioration   89
Preservation Experts and Organizations   90
Preventive Measures   91
Treatments for Damaged Materials   92

Digital Projects   94
Disaster Preparedness   96
Conclusion   98
Review Questions   98

Chapter 9. Trends and Issues   **101**

Trends   101
Issues   102

Suggested Readings   **105**

Index   **109**

Preface

Budgetary constraints and the computerization of library functions and routines have changed the composition of library personnel forever. Library technicians are being hired to replace librarians in many library areas, particularly in technical services. The education and training of library technicians has not kept up with this trend, which leaves a necessary component of a successfully operating library lacking.

Library technology programs have been established to help fulfill this need. However, not only are not enough programs in place in the United States to educate and train library technicians, but also, in the more than forty-four programs that exist today, faculty has a difficult time finding suitable textbooks for the appropriate courses. Most texts in the field of library science have been written for graduate students in a master's in library science program with an emphasis on history, theory, and management. In library technology programs, the faculty must resort to researching a variety of related or unrelated reference materials and then composing a course that caters to the needs of library technicians, with an emphasis on the practical, technical, and electronic aspects of library tasks.

It is with this scenario in mind that I started to assemble books intended for library technicians. This book is designed as a text for the introduction to technical services course in the two-year library technology associate degree or one-year certificate program. The text also will serve as a general reference for library technicians working in the technical services area or interested individuals who would like to learn about what goes on behind the scenes in the library world.

I would like to acknowledge the assistance of my friend Joanne Fontanella. Without her editing skills and encouragement, the task could not have been done so smoothly. I am very grateful to her and thank her for her patience.

Mary Liu Kao

Chapter 1

Introduction

TERMINOLOGY

librarian: The library worker who has a master's degree in library science (MLS) is called a librarian. The librarian represents the upper-level portion of the library personnel hierarchy, usually with a title such as director, assistant director, department head, reference librarian, cataloger, serial librarian, system librarian, etc.

library technician: In the middle level of the library personnel hierarchy, the library technician may work in any area of the library, especially in the technical services area, which includes acquisitions, cataloging, and other responsibilities. Library technicians usually report to librarians and may work alone or may supervise library clerks. The recommended educational level for library technicians is a two-year college associate degree or a certificate in the field. The library technician is also called the library technical assistant, library assistant, paraprofessional, library aide, library associate, library support staff, and library/media technical assistant.

public services: Library work that involves direct interaction with the public, serving the library user directly, is called public services. Functions such as circulation, information, reference, and sometimes interlibrary loan are generally included in the public services area.

technical services: Library work that is done behind the scenes and that does not have much contact with the public is called technical services. Functions such as acquisitions, cataloging, classification, physical processing, mending and repairs, gifts and exchanges, preservation, organization of government documents, and serials control are usually tasks handled by the technical services staff.

LIBRARY ORGANIZATION

Keep in mind that not all libraries are organized in the same way. Traditionally, however, libraries divide library functions into two main categories, *public services* and *technical services.* The public services area deals with tasks that are performed directly in contact with the public and is represented by personnel at the information desk helping library users or at the reference desk assisting users with in-depth reference questions or research problems. Because these are the only members of the library staff that library users actually see and meet, to many users, they are the *librarians* or the total library staff. In fact, there is the other part of the library staff, usually more than half in number, who work behind the scenes preparing the library and its collection so that the library is ready to serve the public. The work done in the offices and areas behind the scenes is called technical services, and the people who work there are referred to as technical services staff. Figure 1.1 illustrates how a library usually is organized.

LIBRARY TECHNICAL SERVICES

Most library users are not aware that the collection in a library must be acquired, organized, and prepared before materials can be found on the shelves. Not only must this work be done before any-

FIGURE 1.1. The Library Organization

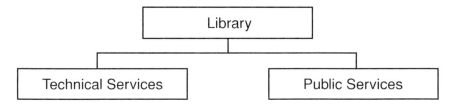

one can use the library and before the public services staff can answer the myriad inquires, but also technical services' responsibilities are a continuing process that goes on day after day. Technical services' activities are accomplished with little interaction with the library users and are performed with the focus on library materials rather than direct, face-to-face involvement with library users.

What library functions and responsibilities are included in the technical services department? Although libraries may have their own distinct ways of dividing library functions and responsibilities, generally speaking the area of technical services includes all the activities related to preparing and making materials accessible to library users. Such works encompass ordering, claiming, and receipt of materials; cataloging and classification; serials control; processing materials; binding, repairs, and preservation of materials; gifts and exchanges; government documents; and database and catalog management (see Figure 1.2). All these functions will be discussed in detail in the following chapters.

In automated libraries, the line may be blurred between technical services and public services because the same databases are maintained and used by both departments. For example, more and more libraries consider circulation or access management part of technical services. In this text, only traditional components are discussed, where circulation and interlibrary loan functions, beyond the scope of this book, remain a part of public services.

FIGURE 1.2. Library Technical Services

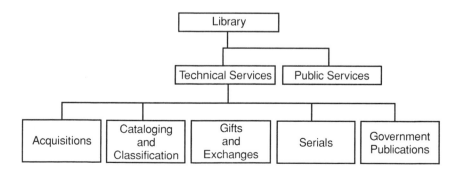

LIBRARY PERSONNEL

Historically, library personnel are divided into two categories: *professional* and *supportive*. Throughout the years, as library work has become more complicated and required skills have become more sophisticated, the library personnel hierarchy has modified the job description for personnel at all levels within these two categories.

The only official guidelines for classification of library staff come from the American Library Association in a document titled *Library Education and Personnel Utilization,* published in 1976 by the American Library Association in Chicago. In this statement, categories of library personnel and their qualifications are defined, requiring that the librarian have a master's degree in library science, the library associate have a bachelor's degree, and the library technical assistant have two years of college level study. At this time, the interpretation of the phrase "two years of college level study" tends to mean an associate degree or a one-year certificate. Clerks are also included in the supportive category, but they are not required to have college training. Figure 1.3 shows the library personnel hierarchy as defined by the American Library Association.

LIBRARY TECHNICIANS

Although no universal title exists for this category of library staff, in this text a library technician is defined as a library staff member who does not have a master's degree in library science, and who performs library functions that require library-specific skills . About 70 percent of all library workers in the United States are library technicians, also referred to as library technical assistants, paraprofessionals, library assistants, support staff, paralibrarians, and library aides. Presently, no qualifying education level exists. However, as more library technicians acquire a college education, it is only a matter of time before the American Library Association will decide on a standard, most likely in the form of a two-year associate degree or a one-year certificate.

FIGURE 1.3. Library Personnel

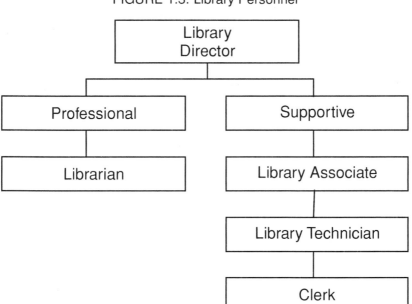

Over the years, because of budgetary restraints and the rapid development of automation, library technicians have assumed increasingly responsible and complex assignments. Many library tasks formerly performed by librarians have become the responsibility of library technicians. Recently, the issue has not been so much a shortage of librarians or the lack of an adequate budget but rather the concern of the library administration is to better utilize the knowledge and skills of librarians and library technicians to provide a more efficient and wider range of library services. This objective has contributed to more interesting and fulfilling career possibilities for those who choose to work in the library world.

With the increase in demands and the expansion of responsibilities, in addition to in-house training, formal education and training have become more important for library technicians. Learning on the job is not sufficient because with automation and new systems being introduced, tasks need to be revised and updated continual. With specific courses, on the other hand, one not only learns the subject matter and acquires general knowledge but also develops the ability to make good decisions and sound judgments in everyday situations. Community colleges all over the United States, Canada, and Australia are responding to the problem by establishing library technology programs for the sole purpose of educating and training competent library technicians. Currently, in the United States, there are forty-four such programs offered in twenty-one states, with some programs offering distance learning courses through the Internet. These programs cannot meet the demand for the vast number of library technicians needed, leaving many libraries with technicians who do not have a formal degree or certificate and for whom training must be acquired in workshops, at seminars, through on-the-job training, and at conferences. As an increasing knowledge of technology becomes essential, a higher level of skills and understanding is necessary. Many professionals in the field have suggested that some kind of certification for library technicians be established as an educational standard, so that the claims that library technicians are professional workers can be justified.

Library technicians are actively involved in professional library activities. From the names chosen for the organizations, it is clear that these are professional groups with high professional interests. Notice that titles for library technicians are far from uniform. In Alabama, the Paraprofessional Round Table is part of the Alabama Library Association. In California, the group called Support Staff is a regular part of the California Library Association. In Colorado, the organization is called the Paralibrarian Division. A survey was done in Fall 1998 showing that Library Technical Assistant is their preferred term. The full report titled "A Study of Library Assistant Positions in Connecticut Libraries" is available on the Connecticut State Library home page at <www.cslib.org>. In Minnesota, the organization is called Support Staff and Paraprofessional Interest Section. According to a nationwide survey conducted by the *Library Journal* in 1995, the largest number of respondents' title was listed as library assistant, followed by library technical assistant. The American Library Association calls its newly established interest group for library technicians Support Staff Interests Round Table, yet in its document published by the Committee on Library Education Task Force for Review of the

American Library Association, *Criteria for Programs to Prepare Library/Media Technical Assistants,* the name library/media technical assistant is used. *The Encyclopedia of Careers and Vocational Guidance* (2000) and the *Occupational Outlook Handbook* (U.S. Department of Labor, 2000-2001) both use the term library technician. The ALA Web page <http://www.ala.org/ssirt/> provides more information on this topic.

The Council on Library/Media Technicians (COLT) is the national organization for library technicians. Besides providing information, it serves as an advocate for the status of library technicians, sponsors conferences and meetings, promotes the education of library technicians, and is involved in activities of concern to library technicians. The COLT Web site is located at <http://library.ucr.edu/COLT/>. There is a Library Support Staff Resource Center home page <http://www.library.ucv.edu/COLT/> that offers a variety of information related to library technicians. Also, many library technicians are actively involved in discussions on various issues in a library support staff listserv called LIBSUP-L. To subscribe, e-mail may be sent to <listproc@u.washington.edu>. There is also a Web site that includes information on listservs in all areas of library work and instructions on how to subscribe; the URL is <www.itcompany.com>.

Two professional journals are published solely for library technicians. One is a bimonthly publication titled *Library Mosaics.* The other is called *Associates: The Electronic Library Support Staff Journal,* which is only available in electronic format. Its address is <www.ukans.edu/nassoc/>. To subscribe, send e-mail to <listproc@ukans.edu>.

Many issues are of great concern to library technicians and are under discussion currently, including the certification issue, inadequate education and training programs, lack of continuing education opportunities for professional growth, low salary, and the absence of a career ladder for promotion.

Library technicians have come a long way from the time they were first recognized and accepted thirty years ago. The March 15, 2000, issue of the *Library Journal* featured its first annual paraprofessional of the year award honoring a worthy candidate, giving a significant boost to the status of library technicians. Although obstacles still remain to overcome, the skills, enthusiasm, and professionalism of these individuals have become an essential part of the library operation, and their contribution to the library community is substantial.

LIBRARY TECHNICIANS IN TECHNICAL SERVICES

Technical services is one area of the library that extensively utilizes the skills and experience of library technicians. Acquisitions, for example, involves tasks that are usually performed by library technicians and clerks. Library technicians receive requests from selectors, obtain items and publication information, create order forms, send orders to vendors or publishers, receive materials, check in materials, and forward invoices to the accounting department for payment. Also, library technicians supervise clerks and assist in communicating with the collection development staff, book vendors, and publishers. In the electronic environment in which libraries subscribe to bibliographic utilities, copy cataloging is done universally by library technicians. Although some libraries continue to have librarians perform original cataloging, library technicians may be assigned to perform original cataloging, as well. In many libraries, the responsibility of the maintenance of databases is assumed by library technicians, and the physical processing of materials is done by library technicians or clerical workers under a library technician's supervision. These duties include ownership stamping, attaching spine labels, inserting security strips, attaching "date due" slips, and whatever may be needed to get the materials ready to be shelved. Other areas such as book repair, preservation, and gifts and exchanges also engage the skills and resources of library technicians.

REVIEW QUESTIONS

1. What are the qualifications for library technicians?
2. What is the recommendation of the American Library Association for the library personnel hierarchy?
3. How is a library organized?
4. What is technical services?

Chapter 2

Computers in Technical Services

TERMINOLOGY

application program: The computer software that constitutes a specific program. Each program has a particular purpose, such as a computer game to be played for leisure, a word processing program, spreadsheet operation, database management, computer graphics, or electronic mail and communications.

automation: System and working procedures that employ computers rather than people to do required tasks. Some initiation device or instruction is assigned and the work proceeds automatically to its conclusion.

integrated system: A library automation system that includes a circulation module, a cataloging module, an acquisitions module, and a serials module. All functions share a single database. It is a more economic and efficient way to operate an automated library, as compared to a single-function system that addresses only one function—acquisitions, for example.

operating system: Computer software used to coordinate the computer hardware with the program and to make it work. The system stores and retrieves data and keeps track of storage space.

turnkey system: A package for library automation that includes hardware, software, maintenance of hardware and software, general system support, initial installation, staff training, subsequent software upgrades, general advice, and troubleshooting methods, all provided by the same vendor.

COMPUTERS

Thanks to developments that made computers smaller, cheaper, and easier to use, the automated library has become commonplace. The emergence of microcomputers and CD-ROM technologies have greatly enhanced computer applications in all library functions. Although it is not necessary to understand programming or other technical information to be able to operate library computer applications, some basic, general knowledge about computers helps to appreciate fully the extensive role of technology.

In the computer revolution, the Internet has emerged as the most important entity not only for information transfer but also as a business tool. This also applies to library system operations, making it possible for libraries to have a Web-based online public access catalog.

Types of Computers

All computers, whatever the size, operate by the same logic. The difference is that size dictates memory storage capacity and speed of processing. Depending on size, there are five types of computers.

Supercomputers are the largest and the most powerful computers. They are used by government agencies and large research organizations that need instant results for the computation and analyzation of huge amounts of data.

Mainframe computers are powerful and have the capacity to process mass information quickly. They are used for number crunching in large-scale computational problems and for archiving large amounts of data, which cannot be handled by smaller computers. Big systems such as the Online Computer Library Center (OCLC) depend on such computers.

Minicomputers are multiuser computer systems on a smaller scale than mainframes. The medium-sized central processing units (CPUs) in minicomputers can process data from many libraries simultaneously and quickly. Many terminals can be connected to the minicomputer's central processing unit, which eliminates the need for individual CPUs for each terminal. Most library automation systems run on minicomputers.

Microcomputers are the most commonly found computers in offices and homes. Microcomputers are called desktop computers because they can be used easily on regular desks, unlike the minicomputers or mainframe computers that occupy more space and need special treatment, such as temperature control. The two kinds of microcomputers that are available on the market now are personal computers (PCs) and Macintosh. Both are capable of performing functions as complex as running an automated system for small libraries. In recent years, microcomputers have been augmented by new technologies and developed into what are called workstations. For example, the cataloger's workstation will consist of the microcomputer with the database software and files installed, plus all the online reference tools that are constantly needed for cataloging, such as the *Library of Congress Classification Schedules, Library of Congress Subject Headings*, and *Anglo-American Cataloguing Rules*, Second Edition, 1998 Revision.

Laptops are very small microcomputers that weigh only a few pounds. They use a rechargeable battery that makes it convenient for users to carry for business use or pleasure. Storage capacity of laptops is as large as that of microcomputers.

Computer Components

Computers have two parts: the hardware and the software. *Hardware* is the machinery, usually referred to as the equipment. *Software* refers to the programs that include the operating systems and the application programs. Both computer hardware and software needs change often and need to be updated regularly.

Hardware

Following is a description of all the components of hardware that together make applications work.

The *central processing unit,* usually referred to as the CPU, is the brain of the computer that holds commands and technical processing information. The central processing unit contains a hard disk drive that allows storage of data entered by the user or that was entered through library activities. Information can also be copied or saved onto floppy disks. Another storage medium in the

CPU is the CD-ROM, which has the capacity of storing an enormous amount of information on one disc. The stored instructions in the CPU make it possible for the computer to handle characters, graphics, and send information to the printer. For important data storage, a backup is necessary, containing duplicate information to prevent the loss of data in case of power failure or computer breakdown. The capacity and speed of the computer are governed by the CPU's internal architecture, called bytes.

The *keyboard* has letters and numbers similar to a typewriter keyboard plus a set of function keys which allows the computer to perform special functions according to the software being used. This is where you input the information you want the computer to process. The keyboard is connected to the CPU by a special cable.

The *monitor* is also called a display screen or terminal. It looks like a television screen and is where the information is displayed. Monitors tilt so that they can be adjusted to make it more comfortable for users. Special cables are used to connect the monitor to the CPU.

A *printer* is the standard hard-copy output device. The printer must be compatible with the program and configured to the CPU.

In order to connect with other computers, a computer needs a *modem*. A modem connects the telephone, the computer, and a telecommunications program so that one computer can communicate with another, and, therefore, one can search databases no matter where they are located. The modem usually is built in, but external modems are available that can be connected to the computer system.

Software

Software is defined as programs that enable a computer system to perform specific tasks. Software is written with instructions in machine language to make the hardware work and to allow the system to carry out complex tasks.

Two different kinds of software are needed to operate a computer: an *operating system* and an *application program*. The available operating systems are Windows, Windows NT, DOS, UNIX, NetWare, and Linux. This is the software that makes it possible to keep the operation active, to communicate with the CPU. A good operating system is user-friendly. The application program contains instructions informing the CPU what to do. Thousands of application programs are available. The basic application programs are word processing, such as WordPerfect or Word; spreadsheet operations such as Excel; data management such as Access; and programs with graphic capacities such as PowerPoint or Print Shop.

Figure 2.1. diagrams the components of a computer system.

LIBRARY AUTOMATION

Technology has shifted the patron's expectations, changing the library's role from a collection of materials to an information provider and mediator.

Computers are used in libraries to perform clerical duties; to produce a wide variety of products, such as bibliographic lists and all sorts of statistical reports, including catalog records; and to help in many activities, such as circulation. Furthermore, computers are used to promote the sharing of catalog records worldwide, saving time and effort for countless libraries.

FIGURE 2.1. Components of a Computer System

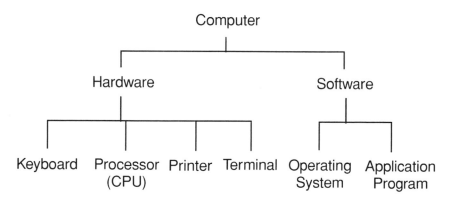

An obvious feature of an automated library is an online catalog in which all of the library's collection is stored in a database and available on a computer. Library users can not only find materials in the library by searching the author, title, or subject (similar to the card catalog search), but also may use many new features as they are made available in the automated environment. This includes more searching strategies, such as keyword and Boolean searching, linking of other databases to offer more materials and information, and linking the online database to automated circulation, cataloging, and acquisitions systems. Furthermore, the online catalog has the capacity of providing full text indexing. Electronic books and journals can also display in full text on the online catalog.

In general, libraries approach the automation issue in two ways: using the *turnkey system* or the *single-function system*. The turnkey system is a complete system composed of all library functions using the same database. Typically, it includes a circulation module, a cataloging module, an acquisitions module, and a serials module. The library purchases from the vendor not only the system but a package that includes hardware, installation, staff training, subsequent software upgrades, troubleshooting help, and system consultation. On the other hand, smaller libraries—most likely school libraries—may purchase a single-functon system to meet their needs. Some examples of single-function systems on the market now include Super Circulation Control with Carder, On-Line Catalog with Carder, Periodical Manager, and Item Inventory and Tracking.

A few years ago, only libraries with a substantial budget could afford to automate their library operations. Recently, thanks to federal and state technology grants and private donations, such as those from the Bill and Melinda Gates Foundation, tens of thousands of even the smallest libraries are automated.

AUTOMATION AND TECHNICAL SERVICES

Although all library functions have been affected by the use of computers, the technical services area has changed most.

Traditional card preparation has become database management. Catalogers who previously spent hours doing original cataloging or searching in bibliographic listings such as *The National Union Catalog* published regularly by Library of Congress now find such cataloging information online in the OCLC, RLIN, and UTLAS databases. In a majority of cases, cataloging has become a quick process in which a record is downloaded for local use without much alteration. If the library is a part of a consortium, its holding symbol is attached to the record, which is already in the database, and the cataloging task is done. This development has prompted the current situation: cataloging costs have been reduced, cataloging staff has switched from librarians to library technicians, and, because one record is utilized by thousands of libraries, uniformity has resulted as strict standards are adhered to. All clerical functions are eliminated. The need for knowledgeable manipulation and maintenance of these databases has significantly increased the visibility of technical services, as the cataloging done behind the scenes becomes instantly accessible in the public catalog to thousands of library users.

For acquisitions, once the information on titles is keyed in or downloaded from another database, it is sent electronically to vendors. The same data stays in the database with an additional note indicating that the material is on order, the date it was ordered, and any other important details. When the item is received, the status of the item in the database is indicated by a word change, from "on order" to "in process," and any other necessary description. The same file is used over and over with little additional input from staff. All the files that contain duplicated information in the manual system are eliminated. The same bibliographic record is used in cataloging. Automation has changed the acquisitions function from being repetitive and tedious to being a quick, efficient process.

The goal of automation in technical services is to increase productivity, to eliminate duplicated effort in organizing materials, to increase the efficiency of operation, and, eventually, to enhance library services. In an automated technical services operation, productivity will be increased. With the same number of staff, more tasks can be accomplished, and they can be done better. The maintenance of the catalog is a good example. With the card catalog, cards need to be printed, alphabetized, and filed in the catalog. For withdrawn materials, all cards need to be removed from the card catalog, one by one—again, a labor-intensive job. Along with the mechanics of updating and correcting a card system are the constantly changing and modifying of cataloging rules. Automation solves these problems completely. The information must be input once, then the computer takes care of the tedious jobs of indexing and filing, saving staff time to work on more meaningful tasks. In an automated catalog, human mistakes are exposed instantly, allowing correction measures to be taken quickly, resulting in a more accurate database and enabling the library to maintain a more efficient and effective technical services organization.

Because of the collective use of the integrated automation system, libraries are able to share resources. For example, original cataloging, which used to be the emphasis of a library technical services operation, has been almost eliminated. Most library materials are now copy cataloged, meaning that the cataloging needs to be done only once, usually by the Library of Congress or other large university or research library. All other libraries can take the information and attach a local record to it, saving hundreds of libraries not only staff time for redundant work but also staff expertise.

The computer revolution has had an overwhelming impact on libraries. Automation has become a fact of life in the library technical services area. Most libraries now use computers for at least part of the technical services operation, be it accessing national or regional databases for cataloging, linking directly to vendors for acquisitions, or using the complete integrated automation system, all of which facilitate the work in both technical services and the public services areas.

REVIEW QUESTIONS

1. What is automation?
2. Why were technical services functions automated before public services?
3. What are the advantages of automating a library operation?
4. What is the difference between an application program and an operating system?
5. What is a turnkey system?

Chapter 3

Bibliographic Utilities and Networks

Cooperation and resource sharing always have been a library tradition. That tradition has continued as automation has taken its prominent place on the scene. The recently introduced terms *library consortia, integrated systems, international networks, shared databases, Internet,* and *World Wide Web* all reflect the interaction and cooperative effort that the development of automation has fostered within the library community.

The Library of Congress has played a leadership role in the history of library automation. Since the 1960s, the Library of Congress has produced and distributed MARC tapes to the library world. MARC stands for *machine readable cataloging,* and MARC tapes contain bibliographic records of all the cataloged titles in the Library of Congress. Each record contains the complete bibliographic information of the title, cataloged with standard cataloging tools. Today, most bibliographic utilities, commercial vendors, and library consortia subscribe to and use MARC tapes as the foundation for their own databases. Information for the same titles can be copied, and items that are not found on the MARC tapes are cataloged by sites, using the same standards (called MARC format) established by the Library of Congress and the library communities. MARC tapes represent a giant step forward in shared cataloging. Understanding the structure and the importance of the MARC format is essential for library technicians working in any area in the library. More will be discussed about the MARC format in Chapter 5 of this text.

TERMINOLOGY

authority records: In an automated system, in order to be consistent with names and subject terms, an established list is used as a standard of accepted values. New information to be entered must be validated against this list; this function is called *authority control*. The records on the list of accepted values are called *authority records*.

bibliographic utility: An organization composed of many member libraries that provides large online databases of bibliographic records which member libraries can use for copy cataloging and other purposes. Participating libraries can use the records and can also contribute to the database by creating new records.

MARC format: Machine readable cataloging information done according to a fixed format. For each element in the bibliographic record, the MARC format specifies a tag number, two indicators, and the field and subfields. For example, for author, the tag number is 100, the first indicator is 1, the second indicator is a blank, and in the field is the author's last name, comma, and then the author's first name. The birth date of the author is placed in the subfield.

MARC tapes: Machine readable computer tapes with bibliographic information produced by the Library of Congress, composed of all the acquisitions of the Library of Congress. Libraries, vendors, and library consortia subscribe to the tapes as a base for performing copy cataloging. The tapes constitute the catalog of the Library of Congress and therefore are used for identifying its collection.

network: Computers connected together to facilitate communication and resource sharing. Networks make it possible for computer users to access information that is not stored into the local database. The term is also used to represent a group of libraries organized together using or forming a bibliographic utility.

retrospective conversion: When a library becomes automated, the existing collection that is indexed in the card catalog must be converted into machine readable form (the MARC format) and stored in a database that will become the online catalog. The titles are entered into the database one by one. This process of building the library database is called retrospective conversion or retrocon for short. It is an expensive and time-consuming process. Some libraries try to do the task in-house, while others outsource the job to vendors.

server: The computers that store the needed information for a network are called servers. The server may be the size of a desktop microcomputer or may be as large as a mainframe computer. The other end of the server is the **client**—the user's computer that asks the server to provide information.

World Wide Web: An Internet facility that links documents from anywhere in the world. The Web document, called a Web page, is linked to other Web pages so that users can jump from one page to another whether it is local or from a remote site. The Web provides a point-and-click interface to access the collection of all online information, and can be accessed via an Internet browser such as Netscape Navigator or Internet Explorer. The Web is also a multimedia showcase that allows video, audio, and videoconferencing over the Net.

Z39.50: A protocol designed for search and retrieval from information systems in a network environment. Use of this protocol in integrated library systems allows different systems to interchange information. It enables the local system to connect to and retrieve data from a remote site by using local menus. For example, with Z39.50 software installed, a library's catalog can be accessed by any users anywhere in the world, even though different automation systems are used.

BIBLIOGRAPHIC UTILITIES AND NETWORKS

Bibliographic utilities are agencies that are composed of many libraries with the purpose of sharing a combined online database. Member libraries can retrieve cataloging information from the database and can create new records for the database for the use of other libraries. Bibliographic utilities have thrived because of the assistance they provide in cataloging. Besides offering cataloging information, bibliographic utilities encourage member libraries to share resources and sometimes offer cataloging or other services to members. Bibliographic utilities play a very important role in library automation processes. Almost every library is influenced by bibliographic utilities either as a participant or as an indirect associate through special arrangement.

The three most prominent bibliographic utilities are the OCLC, the RLG, and the UTLAS.

OCLC (Online Computer Library Center)

OCLC, the oldest and the largest of bibliographic utilities, is a nonprofit organization serving over 39,000 libraries in seventy-six countries. It is by far the busiest bibliographic utility in the world. OCLC's bibliographic database is built from a combination of the MARC tapes from the Library of Congress and contributions from the member libraries. More than 46 million items have been cataloged on the OCLC database with a new record being added every 15 seconds. It is estimated that over 90 percent of library acquisitions can be found in the OCLC database. As the necessity of original cataloging diminishes, the trend of using library technicians in the cataloging department increases. The location, verification, and acceptance of cataloging copy have become the library technician's area of responsibility.

Besides being a shared database to facilitate cataloging, OCLC has much to offer the technical services area. Bibliographic Record Notification delivers upgraded OCLC-MARC records to the subscription libraries, including records with table of contents data. RetroCon is a customized retrospective conversion service for libraries of all sizes and budgets. TechPro offers off-site cataloging and processing services to libraries. PromptCat provides fast copy cataloging for libraries by working on titles with a direct connection to vendors who supply materials to the libraries. New services are added from time to time. More specialized services provided by OCLC include the AsiaLink, a collection-development service that selects and acquires books in Chinese, Japanese,

Korean, and Vietnamese. For more information on OCLC and its services, visit its Web site at <www.oclc.org/>.

RLG (Research Libraries Group)

RLG is a nonprofit membership corporation of universities, archives, historical societies, national libraries, and other institutions. Its database, called RLIN, contains millions of items suitable for research collections. Unlike OCLC, which attempts to meet the varied needs of many types of libraries, RLG is designed to meet the needs of large research libraries only. Membership includes 164 institutions worldwide. Services offered by RLG include information delivery, record supply, interlibrary loan, cataloging, and archival processing, etc. For more information about the RLG, check its Web site <www.rlg.org/>.

The Internet

The Internet is a large network made up of more than 100,000 smaller commercial, academic, and government networks in over 100 countries. It is referred to as a worldwide information highway, providing information on every conceivable subject.

The Internet has become widely used only in the past few years, but, already being "online" has become essential to everyday business functions. Being *online* means being electronically connected to other computers and using the World Wide Web (WWW), a protocol of Internet operation. The WWW is used for retrieving information from local databases or from bibliographic utilities. It can also be integrated with the Z39.50 server and client and search multiple databases simultaneously for information for cataloging or acquisitions.

Web-based technology has caused a sharp decline in demand for closed, proprietary software. Ease of use and especially the convenience of online access to electronic information and data have influenced library automation vendors to develop more Web-based point-and-click systems, replacing the old menu-driven systems.

NETWORKS AND LIBRARY COOPERATION

With the proliferation of library automation and with library users having more sophisticated computer skills, no single library is well enough equipped to accommodate its own users. Cooperation among libraries has become more important and has encouraged the significant growth of consortia, which assist libraries in joint purchasing, interlibrary loan, database sharing for cataloging, and the use of the same automation system.

International and national: The previously described OCLC, RLG, and UTLAS are networks of international nature and membership.

Regional: OCLC has eighteen regional network affiliates that service different regions in the United States. Examples include NELINET, serving over 500 libraries in the six New England states, and AMIGOS, serving the Southern states.

State and local: The development and the popularity of the Internet and resource sharing in libraries have resulted in more consortia being formed within states and locally. Melvyl, a combined catalog in California, serves all University of California campuses. Ohiolink involves seventy-nine higher education institutions in Ohio, sharing the same automation system. Then there are local consortia, such as LION, a network of twenty-two public and academic libraries throughout southeastern Connecticut sharing the same database, and Greater Cincinnati Library Consortium, a consortium of forty-nine academic, public, school, and special libraries.

INTEGRATED AUTOMATION SYSTEMS

Integrated library systems encompass a variety of library operations. By sharing the same database, one computer system can serve several modules for applications in cataloging, acquisition, serials control, circulation, and the online public access catalog. One input or update keeps the entire database current for all functions. The system also allows the online public access catalog to link to the commercially available online reference services such as abstracting, indexing, and full-text reference databases.

Many commercial vendors design and sell integrated library systems to libraries. The majority of vendors offer a complete packaged system—turnkey system—which supplies hardware, software, installation, training, and continuing support. Once the system has been purchased and installed, libraries can start using its functions immediately. Some vendors include *epixtech inc.*, CARL, DRA, Geac, Innovative Interfaces, Sirsi Corporation, Winnebago, and many other smaller ones. Most of these systems have similar functions and are organized by modules. Libraries may purchase the circulation module, cataloging module, acquisitions module, and serials module all together or separately. They are mostly Web-based systems that harness the power of the Internet using programming languages such as HTML, XML, and Java, providing libraries with tools for effortless management of library functions. Systems also use graphical user interfaces (GUI). According to a survey by *Library Journal* in 2000 and published at <www.libraryjournal.com/automated-marketplace>, estimated library systems revenues for 2000 were $440 million. To learn more and to get up-to-date information about the individual system, consult the yearly April 1 issue of *Library Journal,* which reports on an annual survey titled "Automation System Marketplace." In the future, more libraries will outsource systems support and services to an application service provider (ASP) who will maintain servers and software for different customers at a centralized location.

DATABASES

In addition to the system software, databases, provided by database companies and vendors, contain information and data, such as periodical indexes, abstracts, or full text, or they focus on special subject fields, such as the Chemical Abstracts Service. Selecting the appropriate databases for the individual library is an important undertaking and is usually the job of the reference department.

REVIEW QUESTIONS

1. What is the difference between a bibliographic utility and a network'?
2. What are the advantages of participating in a consortium?
3. Name five integrated library systems that are commercially available.
4. What is Z39.50?

Chapter 4

Acquisitions

The acquisitions unit is an important branch of the technical services department. It is the first and the most fundamental process within the library work flow. Although libraries may be organized differently, acquisitions is almost always included in the technical services department, and the tasks involved in acquisitions are performed primarily by library technicians.

Acquisitions encompasses a variety of tasks. Generally speaking, included are bibliographic searching and verification, ordering, claiming, and receipt of materials. Some libraries may add more tasks to the acquisitions unit, such as collection development and copy cataloging; some libraries may not even have a separate unit called acquisitions. In all cases, libraries needs to acquire materials, and the processes involved in acquiring materials remain more or less the same. In this chapter, procedures and tasks related to acquisitions are discussed and explained.

TERMINOLOGY

acquisitions: The processes and systems of ordering and receiving library materials.

approval plan: An agreement between a library and a vendor that allows the vendor to ship a range of titles in a particular subject area designated by the library to the library. Library staff then examines the shipped titles and decides what to keep and what to return to the vendor.

bibliographic information: Information needed to properly identify an item. Such information includes author, title, publisher, publication date, and International Standard Book Number (ISBN).

bibliographic verification: The process of verifying that the bibliographic information is complete and correct.

blanket order: An agreement between a publisher and a library in which the publisher sends all titles published in a certain subject area to the library. The library may not return any title.

collection development: Sometimes this is referred to as collection management; it involves decision making about the collection. A policy on the goals and objectives for the collection is first written, then every task in the department, such as selection of titles, discarding titles, and evaluation of the collection, is done in relation to that policy.

ISBN: An International Standard Book Number is a unique ten-digit number assigned to each book that is published. It looks like this: 1-56024-344-9. The first digit reflects the country of publication. The next few digits denote the publisher and a number the publisher has assigned to each book, and the last digit is a check digit. The number for each book is unique and is used to identify a particular title.

ISSN: Numbers that the publisher has assigned to serials, called the International Standard Serials Number. Similar to the ISBN, the ISSN is a unique number used to identify a particular serial title.

preorder search: Before an item is ordered, it is checked against some identified reference sources to make sure that the library does not already own the item, and that the bibliographic information is complete and correct.

standing order: The library places an order of a particular title with a publisher or a vendor with the understanding that subsequent volumes or issues will automatically be sent to the library. Serials orders are all standing orders. Many reference materials usually have a standing order as well.

vendor: A wholesaler from whom the library materials are purchased. It is synonymous with a book dealer, a jobber, or, in the case of journal subscription, a subscription agent.

weeding: A term that means removing materials from the collection that are out of date, inaccurate, in poor physical condition, or rarely circulated. Weeding is sometimes referred to as collection appraisal.

TYPES OF MATERIALS ACQUIRED

Materials that a library may acquire include but are not limited to printed books, serials, pamphlets, audiovisual materials, electronic formats of books and journals, and computer databases. With all the talk about the "virtual library" and the "virtual collection," libraries will continue, at least in the foreseeable future, to acquire sizable collections in print form. At the same time, the need to acquire more materials in electronic format is increasing.

Books

Books are still the largest part of a collection in most libraries and usually are ordered through vendors or directly through publishers. *Books in Print* is the best source for ensuring that a book is still available. More and more libraries are using online bookstores such as *amazon.com* and *barnesandnoble.com* for quick and inexpensive service.

Pamphlets

The pamphlet file, also called vertical or information file, is an important segment of the library collection. Materials in the pamphlet file include pamphlets, documents, clippings, maps, photocopies, newsletters, annual reports, flyers, pictures, posters, and other information relevant to the library's collection, which may serve the needs of library users. These publications are usually under 100 pages long and, therefore, too flimsy to be cataloged and put on the shelf or too ephemeral to warrant full cataloging. Pamphlet titles can be acquired at no cost or inexpensively from federal, state, and local governments, from chambers of commerce, from tourist bureaus, from foreign embassies, and many other organizations.

Microforms

Microforms are available directly from the publisher or from a commercial company specialized in producing microform materials, such as the University Microfilms International Division of Bell & Howell Information and Learning, where thousands of journal titles are available both on microfilm and on microfiche. Journals in CD-ROM format can also be purchased there as the recent trend in the popularity of libraries buying CD-ROMs instead of microforms continues.

Audiovisual Materials

Audiovisual materials are still very popular with library patrons, especially in public libraries. The sources for finding films, videos, and other types of audiovisual materials are printed or online reference lists and also individual producers' catalogs, such as *Directory of Publishers and Vendors, Best Video, Audio Books' Dealers and Publishers, Educational Video Resources, Filmakers Library, Annenberg/CPB Projects, Creative Educational Video Multimedia, Audio Books on Compact Disc, Inc.,* and many others. A Web site that contains such lists is <http://acqweb.library.vanderbilt.edu/>.

Electronic Materials

Acquisitions staff may be required to handle materials in electronic formats such as CD-ROM, e-books (electronic books), and online subscriptions. Both single titles and continuous database services belong in this category. Libraries must provide computer equipment that is compatible with such materials; an extreme example is the netLibrary in Colorado that provides electronic full-text access to over 34,000 scholarly, reference, and professional texts. Purchasing electronic databases involves a licensing agreement that provides libraries with limited access to the databases.

To keep up with new developments in electronic media, one may read book review journals such as the *Library Journal,* which also reviews other types of media, including electronic materials. The library may gain access, but not ownership, to electronic information from remote sites for free or for a fee. Many libraries choose consortium-based licensing, which is the most cost-effective way to provide access to the library users. The Library of Congress provides many free databases on its Web site <http://lcweb.loc.gov/>.

Out-of-Print Materials

For out-of-print materials that the vendor cannot supply, acquisitions staff must contact the publisher first for available copies or may have to enlist the services of out-of-print dealers who can search for the needed titles for the library. An example is Alibris, a company that specializes in finding hard-to-find and out-of-print books. With an Internet connection, information on millions of books can be located from its Web site <http://library.alibris.com>.

COLLECTION DEVELOPMENT

Collection development, where decisions are made on what is to be purchased for the library, has a close relationship to acquisitions function but usually is not considered a part of the acquisitions unit. Many libraries have a separate and independent collection development department or section; sometimes it is a part of reference services.

Besides its own personnel selecting individual items for the library, some services are offered by publishers and vendors that facilitate the work of the collection development area. Such special programs include the approval plan, the blanket-order plan, and the standing-order plan, all of which are explained in this chapter under the Acquisitions Procedures section.

Weeding, or collection appraisal, performed on a regular basis, is another task that is usually done by the office responsible for collection development. Out-of-date materials should be discarded in order not to mislead readers with the wrong information and to make room for new materials. The *Weeder's Digest* is a reference that lists titles that may be weeded out safely. Its Web site is <www.cyberdc.com/librarydynamics>.

PUBLISHERS, PRODUCERS, AND VENDORS

Because materials can be ordered directly from publishers and producers or from a vendor, library technicians working in acquisitions must have some knowledge of available publishers and vendors in order to choose the best materials and to pay the most reasonable prices for them.

With all the talk about the electronic information revolution and a paperless society, individuals and libraries alike continue to buy books in quantity, suggesting that library technicians working in acquisitions need to have adequate knowledge about publishers.

Vendors are also called jobbers or dealers. These commercial companies are formed with the intention of selling books and other materials to libraries and providing several types of services that relate to acquisitions and processing. Libraries order materials through vendors rather than publishers because vendors offer more competitive prices. Vendors also offer customized services, such as cataloging and processing of the acquired materials, so that once received, items can be shelved immediately. Other special services, such as out-of-print searching and foreign-materials ordering, are available as well. With the appropriate interfaces, the library's acquisitions module can be linked to the vendors' databases that contain the bibliographic information for verifying individual titles and, consequently, allow orders to be placed electronically and effortlessly.

The criteria considered for selecting a vendor include the speed of delivery, competitive pricing and discounting, and the flexibility and variety of its customer services.

ACQUISITIONS PROCEDURES

The process of acquiring materials is the same whether ordering a book, a piece of audiovisual medium, a piece of virtual information in a remote database, or a disposable piece that is to be used for only a short time. The request is first collected, the bibliographic information is then verified, and, finally, the material is placed on order.

Order Requests

Collection of order requests is the first step of the acquisitions procedure. In academic libraries, order requests come primarily from faculty or from librarians in the collection development unit. In public libraries, order requests may come from library users and the collection development unit staff.

Bibliographic Verification

The second step in acquiring materials for the library is to do the preorder search, which is also called bibliographic verification. In this process, the library technician needs to search the library's own catalog to make certain that the library does not already own the material. Standard references also need to be searched so that the titles to be ordered have the correct information, including author's name and spelling, title, publisher or producer, edition, price, and International Standard Book Number (ISBN) or International Standard Serial Number (ISSN).

The standard bibliographies to be checked include *Books in Print*, *Books Out-of-Print*, national bibliographies such as the *National Union Catalog*, publishers' catalogs and flyers, and the databases of bibliographic utilities such as OCLC and RLIN. Depending on the library's automation status, *Books in Print* can be found in print format, on CD-ROM, or as an online subscription via SilverPlatter, OCLC, and Ovid Online. In addition to the necessary bibliographic information, *Books in Print* establishes that the material is indeed still in print. After all the titles are verified, a purchase request is prepared.

Ordering

With the prepared purchase request, an order is placed in one of two ways: by the direct use of different publishers or by the use of the service of a vendor. Vendors are used under normal circumstances because they usually give a bigger discount, provide more personal services, and provide extra services such as cataloging and processing. Under certain circumstances, direct orders must be placed with publishers. This happens when materials are available only through direct order, when a rush order is needed, or when the library holds membership in an organization, and, therefore, can acquire materials with special discounts. In communication with publishers, a library uses its Standard Address Number (SAN) to avoid confusion. Like the ISBN and the ISSN, a SAN is assigned to each library by R. R. Bowker, the designated agency. The SAN for each library is listed in the *American Library Directory.*

Orders can be placed in a variety of ways. Traditionally, the purchase requests are typed on forms. Most vendors and publishers also accept telephone orders. For automated libraries using the acquisition module, titles may be ordered electronically. The automated acquisitions system works most efficiently because the bibliographic information is entered once, and the same data is used for ordering, copy cataloging, and record keeping, thus eliminating the many cumbersome files that normally must be kept in the acquisitions office.

Another way to place an order is through the "approval plan." When contracting for an approval plan, the library first is profiled by the vendor, then the vendor will automatically deliver new titles matching the library's interests. After the books are received, the library can make purchase decisions with the books in hand. Inappropriate materials are returned to the vendor.

The "blanket order plan" is yet another way of ordering. In this plan, orders are placed with the publisher for all published titles of a certain area of interest. Titles may not be returned. In such a plan, paperwork is kept to a minimum, and the library knows what to expect and, in addition, receives a large discount.

For continuous publications, libraries usually participate in a "standing order plan." When a new volume of the same title is published, the publisher or the vendor will send the volume to the library automatically, thus saving staff time by eliminating the ordering procedures. The advantage is that the item will be received soon after publication and with a substantial discount.

Some vendors offer lease services. Public libraries may use this service to receive multiple copies of best sellers to meet immediate need. When interest has waned, the surplus of books is returned. The leasing cost is far less than the cost of buying multiple copies of books whose popularity is temporary.

In 1995, OCLC started a PromptSelect service to streamline the acquisitions process in libraries. PromptSelect provides libraries with access to the OCLC Online Union Catalog and R. R. Bowker's *Books in Print,* allowing acquisitions staff to export the ordering information from the PromptSelect database to the local ordering system. The order process is completed effectively by making the preorder search and order preparation an easy one-step task.

In 1999, OCLC started another service called AsiaLink. This is a preselected collection of fiction and nonfiction books written in Chinese, Japanese, Korean, and Vietnamese. All books are available with full cataloging and processing if the library chooses. Programs such as these work especially well with libraries that do not have language specialists but have specific users to serve.

More and more vendors are offering a Web-based book ordering service, which has become the most efficient way to acquire materials. In such a system, a vast bibliographic database is available from which the library can select and order, and books can be shipped quickly. Brodart's Book Express Plus has claimed that libraries can receive fully cataloged, shelf-ready books two days after the initial order. Ingram Book Group and Baker & Taylor recently have announced similar services.

Receiving

Receiving begins with unpacking the shipment. The received items are then checked against the packing slips to make sure that the correct titles have been sent. If any discrepancy is discovered, problems must be solved by communicating with the vendor. Invoices are then approved for payment, and items are checked in and forwarded to the cataloging department for cataloging.

Bookkeeping

For purchasing materials, funds usually are assigned in categories. For example, a certain dollar amount for fiction, a certain dollar amount for nonfiction, a certain dollar amount for children's materials. In the case of academic libraries, division of funds by academic department or by courses being offered would be appropriate, with an additional allocation for reference materials. Another allocation format might consist of designated amounts for printed materials, for audiovisual materials, for computer databases, etc. No matter how the funds are provided and used, immaculate bookkeeping is essential.

Files and Records

In a library that uses a manual acquisitions system, many files must be maintained. They include: the order request file, the standing-order file, the on-order/in-process file, the correspondence file, the approval plan file, the desiderata file, the claim file, the packing slip file, the invoice file, and the cancellation file. Also, bibliographic information of all kinds is kept in the office for reference purposes. The various files are explained further below.

Requests for orders from different sources such as faculty or the collection development librarian are gathered and an *order request file* is formed. Titles in this file are verified to avoid duplicate orders and for getting the complete bibliographic information. After verification, orders are sent to the publisher or the vendor; that is the *on-order file*. When titles are received, a new *in-process file* is formed so that an accurate record of the status of every item exists. When the processing is done, and the item is shelved, and the card catalog or the online catalog is updated with the new item added, the full cycle of acquisitions if finished.

Combined or separate files are kept for titles on *standing order* to avoid duplicate orders, and titles on *blanket order* are separated from items kept on the *approval plan*. Records of communications with the vendor are kept in the *correspondence file*. *Claiming* is necessary when the library has not received the material as ordered, which demands another file. Libraries usually set a time limit, such as six months or one year, for the back-ordered materials to arrive. If within the agreed-upon time limit the order is not filled, a cancellation notice is sent. Cancellation of orders can also be necessary because of accidentally duplicated orders, because of budget problems, or because wrong bibliographic information was sent to the vendor. This record is called the *cancellation file*. Billing records and records of all financial matters are kept in a *billing records file*.

An automated acquisitions system basically has the same structure as the manual system; it may be a stand-alone acquisitions system or a part of an integrated library system. Either way, the automated system uses the same bibliographic record, and changes of status are recorded, such as the date it was ordered, the date it was received, the date it was cataloged, as well as any other necessary information. Of course, all paper files are eliminated, and acquisitions work is less repetitious, more efficient, and more interesting when the system is automated.

GIFTS AND EXCHANGES

Gift sources may be solicited or unsolicited. Solicited gifts include items for the professional collection, items for the collectors' collection, and personal papers and memorabilia of importance. Unsolicited gifts come from well-meaning people who contribute collections of professional interest, publications of organizations, or personal publications. Gifts should be acknowledged in writing, mentioning the quantity and describing the nature of the titles. The library may not estimate the value of the gifts; this is the job of a professional appraiser, approved by the Internal Revenue Service. Titles from the donated collections should be selected by using the same criteria as purchased materials.

Many libraries have exchange arrangements with other libraries in which they mutually share materials without charge. These shared materials may be unwanted or duplicate materials, or they may be new materials of their own publication.

The library should have a written policy on gifts and exchanges. For example, unwanted gifts may be offered to other libraries, may be sold in a library book sale or to a secondhand book dealer, may be given free to patrons, or may be thrown away. Those discarding materials, especially in public libraries, need to be sensitive to the gift givers and to the library's supporters.

Most of the changes that the acquisitions staff has experienced have come with the advent of automation in libraries. Automation has eased the labor-intensive, repetitive work involved in ordering procedures. Bibliographic utilities, automated vendor services, and the integrated library automation systems all have helped to make the tasks of acquisitions less tedious and more enjoyable. Many libraries have combined the ordering and cataloging functions and renamed the unit the bibliographic division.

REVIEW QUESTIONS

1. What are the procedures for acquiring library materials?
2. Explain what the approval plan, the standing-order plan, and the blanket-order plan are.
3. How has the automation system helped library acquisitions function?
4. How should gift and exchange materials be treated?

Chapter 5

Cataloging and Classification

TERMINOLOGY

author number: A letter and number combination assigned to a particular book representing the author. The letter is determined by the first letter of the author's last name, and the decimal number that follows the letter represents the second and latter letters of the author's last name. Combined with the classification number, it forms a unique symbol, notation, or call number, indicating the book's shelf address. The author number assures that the books on the same subject will be shelved side by side, alphabetically, by authors. Author number is also called book number or Cutter number.

bibliographic record: A term used to describe the cataloging information for an item. Elements on a bibliographic record include author, title, publisher, date of publication, physical description of the item, notes, subject headings, and all other pertinent information needed to identify the material. The elements with their proper form are prescribed in a reference tool titled *Anglo-American Cataloguing Rules,* Second Edition, 1998 Revision.

book number: Same as author number.

call number: A combination of a classification number and a letter-and-number code representing the author. Each call number is a unique number through which library users can easily locate needed material on the shelf.

catalog: A list or a record of all the materials in a library or in a consortium of libraries.

cataloging: The process of organizing library materials and making them accessible to library users. Cataloging work includes descriptive cataloging, assigning subject headings, and assigning classification numbers. Cataloging electronic data and information is called metadata.

cataloging in publication: Abbreviated as CIP, it is the cataloging information printed on the verso of the title page of a publication. This information is supplied by the Library of Congress and can be used for the cataloging convenience of libraries.

classification number: The number/letters assigned to a work to indicate its subject. The purpose is to group all like subjects together on the shelves for easy browsing. There are two universally accepted classification systems. Most libraries use either the Dewey Decimal Classification system or the Library of Congress Classification system.

copy cataloging: The cataloger matches the newly acquired material with the cataloging information already completed on a database or other sources by some other cataloger. The information is copied or downloaded onto the local library's database. This is the most efficient way to perform cataloging.

Cutter number: Same as author number.

descriptive cataloging: The first step of the cataloging process which involves describing the material physically and determining the access points. The rules listed in the reference tool *Anglo-American Cataloging Rules,* Second Edition, 1998 Revision, are followed to perform this task.

Dewey Decimal Classification: A system for classifying library materials by subject. The system puts the entire world of knowledge into ten main classes where a three-digit number is used to represent each class. For example, 000 is *Generalities,* 100 is *Philosophy and Psychology,* and so on. Following the three-digit number may be a decimal point after which more digits are added to define the subject specifically.

Dublin Core: New rules devised by the library world to catalog electronic materials. It defines a core set of metadata elements that allows authors and information providers to describe their work and to facilitate interoperability among resource discovery tools. The required elements include subject, title, author, publisher, other agent, date, object type, form, identifier, relation, source, language, and coverage.

Library of Congress Classification: Same idea as the Dewey Decimal Classification system, except that, for representing subjects, instead of the three-digit number, letters or a letter-and-number combination is used. For example, A is for *General Works,* B-BJ is for *Philosophy, Psychology,* and so on.

notation: A number or number-and-letter combination that is prescribed in the classification scheme. A notation is a call number.

original cataloging: A way of cataloging during which all the procedures to catalog an item are done originally, as opposed to copying the cataloging information already done by someone else. The tasks include doing descriptive cataloging, assigning subject headings, assigning classification numbers, and assigning book numbers, all according to the prescribed rules.

subject cataloging: The cataloging process that involves assigning subject headings and classification numbers to materials. For subject headings, the reference tool to use is either the *Library of Congress Subject Headings* or the *Sears List of Subject Headings,* depending on the choice of the library. For classification, libraries use either the *Dewey Decimal Classification and Relative Index* or the *Library of Congress Classification Schedules.*

subject heading: A specified listed term used for library catalogs to describe the subject matter of materials. Only certain terms are acceptable and must be chosen from the *Library of Congress Subject Headings* or from the *Sears Lists of Subject Headings.*

THE CATALOG

The library catalog is a record of the collection of a particular library or of the holdings of many libraries combined. Listed in the catalog are materials of different formats, including books, video recordings, sound recordings, computer disks, serials, slides, and other media. The catalog provides a list that is shared by every aspect of a library's operation and which can be an important resource for other libraries as well. It is important that the catalog is kept up to date with accurate information on the holdings of the library.

Functions of the Catalog

The library catalog serves the following functions:

1. To inform the users of the library's collection; in the case of a combined union catalog, to inform the users of the available materials of multiple cooperating libraries
2. To help users choose the desired materials
3. To provide access to the materials by having the location symbols listed in the catalog

Types of Catalogs

Catalogs come in different types. Historically, five of the most popular types are:

1. *The card catalog:* For over one hundred years and up to the late 1980s, the card catalog was the catalog type most widely used. The card catalog uses three-by-five-inch cards on which bibliographic information about the item is typed or printed. They are filed alphabetically by author, title, and subject in cabinets specially designed for this purpose.
2. *The book catalog:* The book catalog was the earliest form of catalog. It is a handwritten list of all the titles the library has. Later on, computer printouts replaced these handwritten lists.
3. *The COM (Computer Output Microform) catalog:* This catalog of bibliographic records is produced on microfilm or mi-

crofiche. A special microfilm/microfiche reader is necessary to read the information on the microform.

4. *The CD-ROM (Compact Disc Read-Only Memory) catalog:* In this form, information is engraved on a CD-ROM. A computer with CD-ROM playing capacity is necessary for this type of catalog. Many libraries in the late 1980s and early 1990s used the CD-ROM catalog as a substitute for the more expensive online catalog. The CD-ROM catalog is updated on a regular basis, usually quarterly or monthly.

5. *The OPAC (Online Public Access Catalog):* At present, this is the most widely used type of catalog. Using the computer and special software, the library can use the same bibliographic information to place orders as to catalog materials received. The same database as the public access catalog is available. The most current OPAC is World Wide Web based, referred to as the WebOPAC, which is gradually replacing the character-based OPAC of the 1990s. The WebOPAC can be customized with graphics, logos, and colors to make it not only an efficient tool but also attractive and easy to use.

ELEMENTS OF A BIBLIOGRAPHIC RECORD

Whatever the style of the catalog, on each bibliographic record, the elements included are the same. Elements are prescribed by a widely accepted cataloging tool titled *Anglo-American Cataloguing Rules,* Second Edition, 1998 Revision. The elements that used to be presented on catalog cards today can be found on the computer screen. The online public access catalog contains the same information that was typed or printed on the card, but its appearance is in accordance with the MARC format, devised by the Library of Congress. Elements included in a bibliographic record comprise the following: author, title, call number, ISBN, LCCN, physical description of material, imprint, notes, subject headings, added author, added title, and other local information deemed necessary by the cataloger.

Figures 5.1 and 5.2 are examples of bibliographic elements in public display format and in MARC format, respectively.

FIGURE 5.1. Bibliographic Elements (Public Display Format)

Author	Smith, Joel, 1925-
Title	**Web page development and management : a SPEC kit**
Imprint	Washington, DC : Association of Research Libraries, Office of Leadership and Management Services, 1999

LOCATION	CALL #	STATUS
East Library	016.78 LIU	CHECK SHELF
East Library	016.78 LIU	CHECK SHELF

Series	SPEC kit ; 246
Note	"June 1999."
	SPEC flyer 246 bound in at front.
	Includes bibliographical references.
	PUBLICATION TYPE: Book
Subject	Libraries Automation.
	World Wide Web.
	Web site development.
	Internet
	Libraries -- Automation
	Computer Graphics
Alt author	Liu, Yaping Pater. Association of Research Libraries. Office of Leadership and Management Services.

CATALOGING

Whether or not a needed bibliographic record is available dictates the way cataloging is done. If the record can be found from other catalogs or from any of the bibliographic utilities, the work of cataloging is made easy by copying the existing information and inserting the needed local data; the cataloging is done. This process is called copy cataloging. On the other hand, if the bibliographic record cannot be found in any source, the cataloger then has to follow the rules, the processes, and the procedures to catalog the item. This process is called original cataloging.

Copy Cataloging

Since the majority of library acquisitions have already been cataloged at the Library of Congress or at some other library, the local library needs only to search for the bibliographic record and adopt the existing cataloging information. Although some libraries adopt the

FIGURE 5.2. Bibliographic Elements (MARC Format)

```
001     42416702
008     000000s1999                            eng  cam
100 1   Smith, Joel, |d1925-
245 10  Web page development and management  :|ba SPEC kit
260     Washington, DC :|bAssociation of Research Libraries,
        Office of Leadership and Management Services,|c1999
500     "June 1999."
500     SPEC flyer 246 bound in at front.
500     Includes bibliographical references.
500     PUBLICATION TYPE: Book
650  0  Libraries|aAutomation.
650  0  World Wide Web.
650  0  Web site development.
650  0  Internet
650  0  Libraries|xAutomation
650  0  Computer Graphics
700 1   Liu, Yaping Peter.|aAssociation of Research Libraries.
        |bOffice of Leadership and Management Services.
800 3   |tSPEC kit ;|t246
```

cataloging information for local use without change, others may make minor changes or modifications to suit their local needs. Copy cataloging is a widespread practice in the library world. It saves personnel, time, and money, resulting in speedier service while maintaining high quality. Copy cataloging should be performed whenever possible.

Information for copy cataloging comes from different sources. They include the Library of Congress, cataloging in publication, commercial sources, bibliographic utilities and networks, and print sources.

Library of Congress

The Library of Congress produces and distributes catalogs with full bibliographic information in print format, in microform, in CD-ROM format, and on computer tape, all used extensively by libraries as a source for copy cataloging. The *National Union Catalog,* published in book form as well as on microfiche and in CD-ROM format, had been the most widely used source for cataloging in the past. Since the majority of libraries are automated now, cataloging records of the Library of Congress on computer disc format, called the MARC (machine readable cataloging) tapes, have become the primary source. Libraries can subscribe to the MARC tapes and, by matching the items to be cataloged to the existing records on MARC tapes and adding local coding to them, cataloging is quickly and easily completed. MARC records have become the original source for cataloging, directly through the use of MARC tapes or indirectly through the use of bibliographic utilities and vendor databases, which originate from the MARC tapes.

Cataloging in Publication (CIP)

In most books published in the United States, cataloging information can be found on the verso side (the back) of the title page. Before a book is published, the publisher sends the galley proofs of the book to the Library of Congress. The Library of Congress catalogs the item within ten days and sends the cataloging information back so that the information can be included on the verso side of the title page of the book at publication. This process is called *cataloging in publication*. It benefits libraries enormously because the information comes with the item and no further searching for cataloging information is necessary. Figure 5.3 displays a sample cataloging-in-publication page.

Because the cataloging in publication is done before the book is published, information on the full physical description cannot be included. The copy cataloger is required to fill in the missing information. The title may be changed at the last minute; a subtitle may be added; the date of publication may be revised; or other changes may occur. When using cataloging in publication as the cataloging source, the copy cataloger must be careful in adopting the printed information that all necessary changes and additions are included.

Commercial Sources

When books and other nonprint media are supplied by commercial book vendors, catalog cards or computer disks may be provided too. For small libraries with limited resources and personnel, ordering fully processed items may be the best way of solving

FIGURE 5.3. Sample Page of Cataloging in Publication

The Haworth Press, Inc., 10 Alice Street, Binghamton, NY 13904-1580

Library of Congress Cataloging-in-Publication Data

Kao, Mary Liu

      Cataloging and classification for library technicians/Mary Liu Kao.
      p. cm.
      Includes bibliographical references and index
      ISBN 1-56024-345-7 (acid free paper).
      1. Cataloging—United States. 2. Classification—Books.

I. Title
Z693.U6K36   1995
025.3'0973—DC20   94-44815
                                                                  CIP

the cataloging problem. Under such circumstances, items are received with a full set of cards or with bibliographic information on tapes that can be downloaded into the library's system. Except for occasional minor changes, very little cataloging work is necessary.

Bibliographic Utilities and Networks

In Chapter 3, bibliographic utilities and networks were discussed. Cataloging resources on the database of a network have been based on the Library of Congress MARC tapes plus the contribution of member libraries. Libraries belonging to a network can match the material to be cataloged to the same title found and displayed on the screen. At this point, the copy cataloger needs only to attach the local item to the bibliographic record by adding the local holding symbol. This is also a convenient and efficient way of cataloging.

Print Sources

For manual, nonautomated libraries, information for copy cataloging can be found in print sources such as *Booklist*. It is used by the acquisitions staff for ordering materials and concurrently provide the necessary information for a bibliographic record.

It is important to remember that in performing copy cataloging, information can be completely adopted only if an exact match is located. Slight variations such as different edition or different binding are not considered an exact match, and, in such cases, information must be altered and modified so that a new entry can be established.

Where original cataloging has continued to be the librarian's responsibility, copy cataloging has fallen to the library technician. The library technician's skills, knowledge, and familiarity with the procedures and sources of copy cataloging are essential for accurate copy cataloging. Occasionally, for items such as locally produced materials for which matches cannot be found in the databases of any local or remote sites, original cataloging must be performed.

Original Cataloging

Although a majority of library materials are cataloged by way of copy cataloging, there are always some materials, such as local government publications, materials in specialized subject fields, publications or productions from private sources, pamphlets, and other types of materials for which matches cannot be found on computer databases. Under such circumstances, the cataloger must perform original cataloging.

Original cataloging means that the cataloging on an item is done by extracting the information needed for the bibliographic record from the material itself, plus using some standard tools to establish other necessary elements. As Figure 5.4 shows, the task of original cataloging is divided into two broad areas, *descriptive cataloging* and *subject cataloging*. Subject cataloging is done in two steps, subject heading and classification number.

Rules and regulations are formulated and published for each step. These rules are used universally by the library world to provide consistency and uniformity. The library technician must be familiar with appropriate cataloging tools that contain these rules so that procedures for specific materials can be followed when

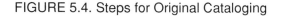

FIGURE 5.4. Steps for Original Cataloging

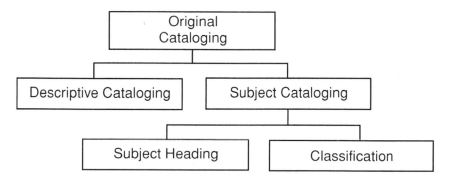

performing cataloging tasks. These reference tools include the *Anglo-American Cataloguing Rules, Second Edition, 1998 Revision, Library of Congress Subject Headings, Sears List of Subject Headings, Dewey Decimal Classification Schedules, Library of Congress Classification and Relative Index,* and *C. A. Cutter's Three-Figure Author Table.* The steps of the cataloging processes together with the tools being used are explained here.

Descriptive Cataloging

The *Anglo-American Cataloguing Rules,* Second Edition, 1998 Revision, is used when performing the first step in cataloging, called descriptive cataloging. Generally referred to as AACR2R in the library world, this volume is a collection of rules adopted by a majority of libraries in the United States, Great Britain, Canada, and Australia. Published by the American Library Association, the AACR2R supplies rules for the physical description of both books and nonbook materials. It also presents rules for establishing the access points for retrieving materials, called the main entries and the added entries. Furthermore, it spells out exactly how bibliographic information is to be transferred onto the card or into the library computer databases. In addition to the print format, AACR2R is available on CD-ROM produced by the Library of Congress, titled *Cataloger's Desktop.* For example, on Figure 5.5, the shadowed areas are elements governed by the AACR2R rules.

FIGURE 5.5. Elements in Bibliographic Record Governed by AACR2R (the Shaded Areas)

Author	Kao, Mary Liu
Title	Cataloging and classification for library technicians / Mary Liu Kao.
Imprint	New York : Haworth Press, c1995.

LOCATION	CALL #	STATUS
East Library	Z693.5.U6 K36 1995	CHECK SHELF

Descript	xii, 137 p. : ill. ; 23 cm.
Series	Haworth cataloging & classification
	Haworth series in cataloging & classification
Bibliog.	Includes bibliographical references (p. 133-134) and index.
Note	English
Subject	Cataloging -- United States
	Classification -- Books
ISBN	1560243449 (acid-free paper)

Subject Cataloging

The second step in original cataloging is called subject cataloging. Subject cataloging is divided into two steps: subject heading and classification number.

Subject heading. In searching for information or doing research, most library users attempt to find materials in a particular field by checking under the appropriate subject. Thus, the task of assigning subject headings to materials takes on great importance. The purpose of assigning subject headings is to list all the materials on a given subject under a uniform term or phrase, so that, in one search, library users can identify all the materials on a certain topic and also can find them side by side on the shelves. A subject heading may be a term, name of a person, group, place, or a phrase. To ensure uniformity, terms to be used for subject headings are listed in two reference sources. When assigning subject headings, the cataloger uses a reference source that lists legitimate terms. *Library of Congress Subject Headings,* designed and constantly updated by the Library of Congress, is the choice of a majority of libraries. Some smaller libraries, especially school libraries or nonautomated libraries, use another similar but less complicated reference tool titled *Sears List of Subject Headings,* published by H. W. Wilson. The shadowed area in Figure 5.6 shows the subject headings in a bibliographic record that have been compiled according to either *Library of Congress Subject Headings* or *Sears List of Subject Headings.*

Classification number. After the descriptive cataloging is done, subject headings are assigned. The next step is to assign the classification number. A classification number places all similar and related subject materials together on the shelves so that library users can more conveniently locate what they want. The classification number, combined with the author number, forms a unique notation, which becomes the location symbol for the material. With this unique notation—called a call number—labeled on the spine, the library staff can easily shelve the material in its proper place after each use.

Several classification systems are designed for adoption by libraries. Two have been universally adopted and are widely used. The Dewey Decimal Classification system is used primarily by public libraries and school libraries, and the Library of Congress

FIGURE 5.6. Subject Headings in a Bibliographic Record (the Shaded Areas)

Author	Kao, Mary Liu
Title	**Cataloging and classification for library technicians / Mary Liu Kao.**
Imprint	New York : Haworth Press, c1995.

LOCATION	CALL #	STATUS
East Library	Z693.5.U6 K36 1995	CHECK SHELF

Descript	xii, 137 p. : ill. ; 23 cm.
Series	Haworth cataloging & classification
	Haworth series in cataloging & classification
Bibliog.	Includes bibliographical references (p. 133-134) and index.
Note	English
Subject	Cataloging -- United States
	Classification -- Books
ISBN	1560243449 (acid-free paper)

Classification system is preferred by academic libraries and special libraries.

Dewey Decimal Classification system. This system divides the entire world of knowledge into ten main classes. The ten classes are divided further into ten divisions, and each division divided into ten sections. All classification numbers are three-digit numbers, such as 100, 140, 589, etc. The first digit indicates the main class, the second digit indicates the division, and the third digit indicates the section. Following the three-digit number is a decimal point after which additional digits may be included that more specifically define the subject. For example, the Dewey Decimal Classification number for a book may be 025.431. Zero, as the first digit, indicates the book is in Generalities class; 2, as the second digit, represents the topic of library and information science; and 5, as the third digit, further indicates that the book is about the operations of libraries, archives, and information centers. The 431 after the decimal point describes the subject even more specifically by indicating that this book is about a classification system called the Dewey Decimal Classification system. The *Dewey Decimal Classification and Relative Index,* a four-volume set, is published and continually updated by the Forest Press, a division of OCLC. In addition to the print version, the *Dewey Decimal Classification, and Relative Index* is also produced on CD-ROM, called *Dewey for Windows,* available from OCLC Forest Press.

Library of Congress Classification system. The Library of Congress classification system divides knowledge into twenty-one broad categories, using a letter to represent each subject field. The letters I, O, W, X, and Y are excluded. Each subject letter may be combined with one or two more letters followed by a numeric value that may have a decimal point and more digits. For example, consider the Library of Congress Classification number HF5549.5. H, in this case, represents social science; HF means the book is about commerce; by adding 5549 it is clear that the book is about personnel management. Adding .5 to the number specifies employment management. Each of the twenty-one subjects is developed separately and therefore has its own separate booklet outlining the details. The Library of Congress Classification schedules are published and maintained by the Library of Congress. Every schedule has its own publication schedule; updated schedules are published from time to time. In addition to the print format, the Library of Congress has produced *Classification Plus,* which is a full-text, Windows-based CD-ROM that contains the *Library of Congress Classification Schedules* and *Library of Congress Subject Headings. Classification Plus* is available as an annual subscription with quarterly issues.

The book number. Whether the Dewey Decimal or the Library of Congress Classification schedule is used, the book number, also called the author number or the Cutter number, must be added and attached to the classification number to make the symbol complete, resulting in a unique notation representing the particular item. There are different ways of assigning the book number. For libraries using the Dewey Decimal Classification system, one way to figure out the book number is to use a reference tool titled *C. A. Cutter Three-Figure Author Table* or a different version of it with the same content, titled *Cutter-Sanborn Three-Figure Author Table,* or a more simplified version of it called *Cutter's Two-Figure Author Table.* For libraries using the Library of Congress Classification system, a simple *Cutter Numbers Devised by LC* is used. Basically, these reference tools all work the same way by taking the first letter of the author's last name and adding a series of numbers to it. The numbers are so devised that materials about the same subject will be arranged alphabetically on the shelves by author, again, for easy browsing by library users. For example, the author number for Samuel Baker is .B177. Note that there is a decimal point before the author number. Therefore, the book with this author number should be shelved as B first and then as .177, digit by digit, not as the whole number 177.

Some school and public libraries do not use the Cutter's reference for assigning author numbers. They simply use the first three letters of the author's last name or the first six letters of the author's last name, depending on the size of the collection. The ultimate goal is the same, that of arranging the materials by subject first, under the same subject, and by the author's last name.

In some cases, more information is added and reflected in the call number. They are called *work marks* and include prefixes such as REF (for reference book), FIC (for fiction), etc., added to the top of the call number, or publication date (such as 2000), volume number, and copy number added to the bottom of the call number. This works the same for both the Dewey Decimal system and the Library of Congress system. A complete call number may look like this: REF 650.14 .L112 2000 V.1 C.1.

On the bibliographic record that is displayed in Figure 5.7, the shaded area shows the classification number and the author number, which together form the call number.

For cataloging electronic information, a set of new rules, called the *Dublin Core,* is applied. *Dublin Core* defines a set of metadata elements that would allow authors and information providers to describe their work. The goal is to simplify the cataloging processes for such ephemeral electronic resources that do not warrant full cataloging. The required elements include subject, title, author, publisher, other agent, date, object type, form, identifier, relation, source, language, and coverage. For more information on the *Dublin Core,* visit its Web site at <http://dublincore.org/>.

This section gives a general introduction on how original cataloging is done and how the result appears. The intention is to give the library technician a general understanding of the process of original cataloging. The information provided here is not sufficient for actually teaching one how to use these reference tools to

FIGURE 5.7. Classification Number in a Bibliographic Record (the Shaded Area)

Author	Kao, Mary Liu
Title	**Cataloging and classification for library technicians / Mary Liu Kao.**
Imprint	New York : Haworth Press, c1995.

LOCATION	CALL #	STATUS
East Library	Z693.5.U6 K36 1995	CHECK SHELF

Descript	xii, 137 p. : ill. ; 23 cm.
Series	Haworth cataloging & classification
	Haworth series in cataloging & classification
Bibliog.	Includes bibliographical references (p. 133-134) and index.
Note	English
Subject	Cataloging -- United States
	Classification -- Books
ISBN	1560243449 (acid-free paper)

catalog. For future catalogers, it is necessary to acquire textbooks that are devoted to the topic of cataloging and classification.

THE MARC RECORD

Whether copy cataloging or original cataloging, knowledge and understanding of the MARC format is essential for catalogers. A MARC record is a machine readable cataloging record. Where catalog card information can be typed onto the card, with automation, information to the computer database must be sent in a way that the computer can interpret the information. The Library of Congress has devised this format, and libraries all over the world have adopted it. Essentially, each area on the card is put under a three-digit number called a tag, which the computer interprets as the code for the element. For example, 100 represents author, while 245 represents title. An example of a MARC record is shown in Figure 5.8.

All MARC records start with tags. Then there are spaces for two possible indicators, each with a numeric value of 0 to 9. Some indicators are left blank, since they are undefined by the Library of Congress. Following the indicators is the description, called a

FIGURE 5.8. A MARC Record

```
005      20000223105748.7
008      941214s1995    nyua      b    001 0 eng   cam a
010      94044815 //r95
020      1560243449 (acid-free paper)
035      |910360426
040      DLC|cDLC|dDLC
043      n-us---
050 00 Z693.5.U6|bK36 1995
100 1  Kao, Mary Liu
245 10 Cataloging and classification for library technicians /|cMary
       Liu Kao.
260      New York :|bHaworth Press,|cc1995.
300      xii, 137 p. :|bill. ;|c23 cm.
490 1  Haworth cataloging & classification
504      Includes bibliographical references (p. 133-134) and index.
546      English
650   0 Cataloging|zUnited States
650   0 Classification|xBooks
830   0 Haworth series in cataloging & classification
```

field. Within each field, there may be several subfields, separated by delimiters. For example, in Figure 5.8, 050 is called the tag, 00 are the two indicators, and Z693.5.U6K36 1995, in this case the call number, is called the field. Within the field, | is the delimiter (in some systems, $ or another symbol is used for the delimiter), and |b indicates that what follows is in subfield b, in this case, K36 1995, the author number and the date.

The copy cataloging staff must know how to read MARC format for easy editing and modifying. The original cataloger must have a thorough detailed understanding of it to ensure that each element of the material is cataloged in the MARC format with the correct tag, indicators, field, and subfields. For a complete explanation of the MARC record and a complete listing of all MARC tags, indicators, fields, and subfields, consult the Web site of the Library of Congress at <www.loc.gov/marc/>.

CATALOGING AND PROCESSING ROUTINES

After materials are received by the acquisitions department and are properly checked in, they are sent to the cataloging department. In some libraries, the two departments are grouped into one, called technical processing or some other name meaning the same thing. Materials are then cataloged as described in this chapter and finally physically prepared so that they can be shelved. The cataloging and processing routines are summarized here:

1. Materials are received and properly checked in.
2. Search database or other sources for copy cataloging information.
3. If information is found, do copy cataloging.
4. If information is not found, do original cataloging.
5. Enter all necessary information onto the database according to MARC format.
6. For nonautomated libraries, card sets for the card catalog are prepared.
7. Prepare the materials physically, including placing spine labels on materials, attaching bar-code labels, attaching secu-

rity strips, adding plastic jackets, stamping ownership stamp in designated places, attaching date-due slips, etc.
8. File catalog cards and shelf-list cards, if used.

Cataloging, especially if the library is a part of the network, must be done according to the discussed rules and format in this chapter so that other libraries can use the records. Every library has its own requirements for processing materials. So that all materials are processed uniformly, library technicians should be familiar with such processing routines of their own libraries and follow the procedures rigidly.

In the technical services area, the tasks of cataloging and classification are the most important library functions. Although they can be time-consuming and labor-intensive duties, copy cataloging has made it more cost effective and efficient for the cataloging staff. Care and precision continue to be essential ingredients in the process, especially as library customers become more adept at using automated devices. Because a small error spontaneously affects an entire network system, refined skills and a broad knowledge are expected from those in the technical services areas, especially in cataloging and classification.

REVIEW QUESTIONS

1. What purposes does the catalog serve?
2. List the elements of a bibliographic record.
3. What are the steps of original cataloging?
4. List and briefly explain the reference tools that are used for cataloging.
5. What are the steps of copy cataloging online using a bibliography utility?
6. What are the advantages of doing copy cataloging?
7. What is a MARC record?

Chapter 6

Government Publications

Title 44 of the U.S. Code is the law that guides the nation's policies on publishing, printing, distributing, and managing government publications. According to Title 44, government publication is defined as "Information matter which is published as an individual document at government expense, or as required by law" (U.S. Code Annotated, 1927). The document may be published by the government itself or by an outside publisher or printer at government expense. The document may be in book form, a serial, audiovisual material, or in electronic format, such as CD-ROM, or online. The term *government publication* usually refers to a publication from the federal government; however, publications from individual states, local governments, foreign governments, and international organizations also are considered government documents.

Some government documents are for the government's administrative or operational use. A large majority of government documents, however, provide authoritative and up-to-date information for individual citizens. Government documents exist in all subject fields and in all areas of knowledge. Sometimes a government publication is the only source of information on a certain topic; on other occasions, it may be the major source of information. In any case, it constitutes a very important segment of a library's collection and is a necessary element in the library technician's area of responsibility.

TERMINOLOGY

Federal Depository Library Program: A program stipulated by U.S. Code Title 44 and sponsored by the Government Printing Office of the U. S. government. In this program, depending on the conditions, certain public, academic, or other types of libraries are chosen to receive government publications at no charge. In return, the libraries must provide to the general public comprehensive and no-fee access to federal government information in all forms. These libraries are called federal depository libraries. There are currently about 1,400 federal depository libraries.

government document: Also called government publication, the item may be on any subject and in any format, but it is published either by the government or at government's expense.

Government Printing Office: A branch of the U.S. government that is given the responsibility to produce documents created by federal branches and offices and to disseminate the produced information through its Sales and the Federal Depository Library Programs. It is the largest printing house in the world. It is commonly known as the GPO.

Superintendent of Documents Classification system: A classification system devised for the purpose of classifying government documents. The system groups publications of the same agency together, rather than grouping according to the same subject, as other classification systems usually do. It uses a letter-and-number-combination to signify the agency, the subdivision of the agency, the type of publication, the date of publication, and other relevant information about the document. It is called the SuDoc system for short.

THE GOVERNMENT PRINTING OFFICE

Established in 1861, the Government Printing Office has become the largest printing house in the world. At the GPO, one of the world's largest volumes of informational literature is disseminated, distributing more than 65 million government publications every year in print, microform, and electronic formats. It services offices in both legislative houses, in the executive branch, and in the judicial branch. Although the GPO does not produce every document created by federal branches and offices, it prints congressional documents and materials that are urgent in nature. Other materials are printed by commercial printers that have a contractual arrangement with the government. When documents are printed by commercial printers, they retain the GPO imprint and are considered government publications.

U.S. Code Title 44 establishes that the Public Printer, a person nominated by the President of the United States with the consent of the Senate, shall be in charge of the Government Printing Office. The Public Printer is responsible to the Joint Committee on Printing, consisting of five senators and five members of the House of Representatives. The U.S. Code states that the Public Printer shall appoint a person, titled Superintendent of Documents, to be in charge of receiving and selling government documents. The responsibilities of the Superintendent of Documents include preparing comprehensive catalogs and indexes for all documents and distributing documents to agencies, libraries, and individuals through Sales and Federal Depository Library Programs.

After the passing of the *Government Printing Office Electronic Information Access Enhancement Act of 1993,* the GPO progressed into the electronic age. The Superintendent of Documents was put in charge of maintaining an electronic directory of federal electronic information, providing a system of online access to the Congressional Record, Federal Register, and other appropriate publications, and operating an electronic storage facility for federal electronic information. Since then, documents have been published and GPO databases have been established for easy access. The electronic storage system makes it possible for the public to access and retrieve older documents, and the system assists in the sale and distribution of newly published materials. This service that enables the public to have free access to electronic materials is called GPO Access. GPO Access is located online at <http://www.access.gpo.gov.> This act also requires that the Superintendent of Documents maintain an electronic directory of federal electronic information, the GPO Locator Service. The GPO Locator Service describes the information it contains, gives referrals to federal depository libraries that hold such information, lists the federal agencies that house the data, and gives information about the GPO Sales Program.

Two avenues for achieving the main purpose of the GPO, which is to disseminate information, are with the Sales and with the Federal Library Depository Program.

Sales

Government publications constitute a very important part of a library's collection. They are inexpensive or often free and encompass special topics about which information is difficult to find in any other type of publication.

The Government Printing Office operates twenty-four bookstores across the country and has a major distribution center in Pueblo, Colorado. Its address is Consumer Information Center, Pueblo, Colorado, 81009. Books, posters, pamphlets, maps, CD-ROMs, and computer disks are available in the Sales Program. In addition to direct sales to bookstore customers, certain documents can be acquired through commercial bookstores, government documents dealers, and jobbers. Mail, fax, telephone, and online ordering are also accepted by the Superintendent of Documents, Government Printing Office, Washington, DC, 20402. The addresses, hours, and maps of all bookstores can be found on the GPO Web site at <http://www.gpo.gov/>.

The Government Printing Office publishes catalogs and indexes to facilitate the selection and acquisition of documents. The *Consumer Information Catalog,* which lists topics of interest to the general public, is published four times a year and is distributed by the Consumer Information Center in Pueblo, Colorado. Many of the listed titles can be acquired with minimal or no charge. More information on the list and its contents is available online at <www.pueblo.gsa.gov>.

A most important catalog published by the Government Printing Office is titled *Monthly Catalog of United States Government Publications.* This catalog covers new titles published by the government on a monthly basis, with a semiannual and annual cumulative index. Titles listed are properly cataloged in MARC format, and contain the bibliographic information along with the Superintendent of Documents Classification numbers and subject headings. It serves not only as a selection tool but also as a cataloging and reference tool. In addition to the main list, there is information on how to order publications; a list of government bookstores around the country; and information on the Federal Depository Library Program, with a complete list of regional depository libraries.

The *Periodical Supplement* is a separate part of the *Monthly Catalog of United States Government Publications* and gives complete bibliographic information for serials, including lists for classification changes, title changes, ceased publications, and periodicals that are now available online.

In addition to the print version, the Monthly Catalog of United States Government Publications is available in CD-ROM format and online. The online version is accessible at <http://www.access. gpo.gov/su_docs/dpos400.html>, is updated daily, and contains the bibliographic records published in the Monthly Catalog of United States Government Publications since 1994.

Federal Depository Library Program

The Federal Depository Library Program was established by the *Depository Library Act of 1962*. There are about 1,400 libraries in the United States designated as depository libraries including public, academic, or other types of libraries. This program's main purpose is to assign designated libraries to receive government publications at no charge, and, in return, the libraries must provide to the general public comprehensive and no-fee access to federal government information in all formats. This has been a successful and valuable relationship for the federal government, the participating libraries, and the general public.

The depository libraries are designated by law or nominated by senators and representatives for their states. There are two types of depository libraries: the *regional depository libraries* and the *selective depository libraries*. U.S. Code Title 44 stipulates that no more than two libraries in each state may be designated as regional depositories, which shall receive all government publications authorized for distribution and shall keep such materials permanently. The regional depository library may be a state library, an academic library, or a public library. On the other hand, the selective depository libraries receive only selected categories of government publications that meet their own needs. The librarians in charge of the government documents usually make the selection from the lists sent to them by the Government Printing Office. The materials in the selective depository library's collection may be discarded after five years. Following are conditions for a particular library to be named a depository library:

1. Every senator may name two libraries in his or her state;
2. Every House of Representatives member may name two libraries in his or her district;
3. A Special Act of Congress may designate a particular library as a depository;
4. All land-grant colleges, service academies, libraries of the government's executive departments are eligible to be named a depository library;
5. The American Antiquarian Society in Massachusetts;
6. The highest appellate court of any state may request that its library be designated as a depository library; and
7. Any accredited law school may request that its library be designated as a depository library.

In the networked environment, with the proliferation of electronic documents published by government agencies, a shift toward a decentralized mode of access to government information is anticipated. Depository libraries not only will have to keep abreast with the technology by providing appropriate equipment for disseminating information, but also will have to keep up with the primary producers of information in the depository program.

SUPERINTENDENT OF DOCUMENTS CLASSIFICATION SYSTEM

As described in Chapter 5, cataloging of materials is done in three distinct steps: descriptive cataloging, subject headings, and classification. The cataloging of government documents is done the same way. For descriptive cataloging, the same rules as for nongovernment titles are followed, as contained in the *Anglo-American Cataloguing Rules,* Second Edition, 1998 Revision. If a title is available only via the Internet, a computer file record is created. If it is available both in print and electronically, the existing record is enhanced by adding a 530 note and a linked URL in the 856 field of the MARC record. Also, as is the case for nongovernment publications, the *Library of Congress Subject Headings* is used for assigning subject headings to government documents. The classification system, however, is different. Whereas, for general nongovernment materials, libraries choose to use either the Dewcy Decimal Classification system or the Library of Congress Classification system, as explained in Chapter 5, for government documents, a system called the Superintendent of Documents Classification system, or SuDoc classification, is used.

In the SuDoc classification system, documents are grouped together by issuing agency, not by subject, as is the case in the Dewey Decimal and the Library of Congress Classification systems. The SuDoc notation consists first of an alphabetical designation representing the issuing government department or agency, followed by a space. After the space, a number represents the subordinate division of the agency. This number is followed by a period, then a number that signifies the type of publication of the document. A colon follows, and, finally, a book number, which may be the volume or issue number of a serial or the date of publication. A few examples of the alpha element for agencies are:

A for Department of Agriculture
C for Department of Commerce
GP for Government Printing Office
J for Department of Justice
SBA for Small Business Administration
T for Department of Treasury
TD for Department of Transportation
X, Y for Congress

After the agency letter(s) comes a number for the subordinate bureau of the parent agency. Number 1 is used for the parent agency, and numbers 2 through 99 are used for subordinate bureaus, administrative offices, etc. For example, A 1 represents the Agriculture Department, while A 13 represents the Forest Service, which is a branch of the Agriculture Department. Sometimes a secondary subagency is also indicated after the period, such as A 13.40. While A 13 is the Forest Service, A 13.40 is a subagency of the Forest Service, the Southern Forest Experiment Station.

After the subordinate agency designation, there is a period. After the period, the next number represents the type of publication, such as:

1 for annual report
2 for general publication
3 for bulletins
5 for laws
6 for rules, regulations, and instructions
8 for handbooks, manuals, and guides
9 for bibliographies, list of publications
10 for directories

This sequence: the agency letter, the subordinate office number, and the type of publication ends with a colon and constitutes the class stem. After that will appear the book number which may be in the form of letters or numbers referring to a volume number, issue number, date, document number, or, for easy and swift identification, a unique letter-and-number combination designation.

In summary, the elements of a SuDoc classification number may include the following:

1. Agency
2. Subordinate bureaus and offices
3. A period
4. Type of publication
5. A slash
6. A colon
7. Individual book number
8. Last three digits of the year for annual publications

Exceptions to the rules include:

1. X is used for Congressional Records.
2. Y 1 is used for House and Senate publications.

3. Y 3 is used for boards, commissions, and committees established by Congress.
4. Y 4 is used for hearings and committee prints.

Following are some examples of SuDoc classification numbers.

- The SuDoc classification number for *Monthly Catalog of United States Government Publications* is GP 3.8/8:998/12.

   GP denotes Government Printing Office.
   3 denotes Library Division, which is a subdivision of the Government Printing Office.
   8 denotes the type of publication as handbooks, manual, and guides.
   /8 denotes that eight issues are published per year.
   998 denotes the year of publication, in this case the year of 1998.
   /12 denotes the month of the publication, in this case the month of December.

- Y 4.W36:105-25 is another example of a SuDoc classification number for a book titled *The Future of Social Security for This Generation and the Next.*

   Y 4 is the designated notation for all hearings conducted by the House of Representatives.
   W36 denotes the Committee on Ways and Means of the House of Representatives.
   105-25 indicates the congressional session.

The SuDoc classification number system is the call-number scheme used in all depository libraries for their federal document collection. Because the classification system is based on the current organizational status of the government author, changes occur as the organizational structure changes. As a result, publications of some issuing agencies may be located at several different places on the shelves.

To accommodate the growing amount of electronic information, the U.S. Government has created the Government Information Locator Service, a decentralized standard for creating metadata. It is still in the developmental stage and has not been completely implemented. The Dublin Core metadata standard is suggested as an alternative approach to cataloging online publications. The American Library Association, the Government Printing Office, the Library of Congress, and some other concerned parties together will decide the future of the cataloging and classification system that should be applied to the online government publications.

It is essential for the library technician to understand what the letters and numbers in a SuDoc notation mean, but the responsibility for actually assigning the SuDoc classification numbers for government documents lies with the catalogers in the Library of Congress and the Government Printing Office, as stipulated by U. S. Code, Title 44. Library technicians will be required to record the SuDoc designation from a reference source such as the *Monthly Catalog of United States Government Publications* or from some other computer databases. In the rare case that an original SuDoc notation needs to be assigned, the reference source The *GPO Classification Manual* is used for instructions. A detailed explanation of the Superintendent of Documents Classification system is available at <http://www.access.gpo.gov/su_docs/dpos/explain.html>.

MAINTENANCE OF GOVERNMENT PUBLICATIONS

Depository libraries that have a large government document collection usually shelve them in a separate government document area for in-house use only, sometimes taking over an entire floor of the library building. When checking in an individual title, the SuDoc number is copied, usually on the upper left-hand corner of the cover, after which the material is shelved in the designated area of the library according to its SuDoc numbers. Libraries that are not depository libraries most likely will acquire some government documents as well. In such cases, there usually is not a separate government document section, and the documents are treated as regular print materials and cataloged under the Dewey Decimal Classification system or the Library of Congress Classification system. They are processed in the same way as other titles and integrated into the regular collection, and may be checked out in the same manner as any other materials in the collection. Furthermore, to provide public access to government documents published only in electronic format, proper and adequate computer equipment needs to be acquired and maintained by the library. For more information and discussion about government publications, the issues involved, etc., library technicians may want to join a listserv organized by government documents librarians, called GOVDOC-L.

REVIEW QUESTIONS

1. What is considered a government publication?
2. What are the responsibilities of the Superintendent of Documents?
3. How are federal depository libraries designated?
4. Explain the Superintendent of Documents Classification system.
5. How are government publications maintained in a library?

Chapter 7

Serials

A serial can be defined as a publication that is issued in successive parts, with the intention of continuous publication for an indefinite period of time. It may be published regularly, such as weekly, monthly, quarterly, annually, etc. It may also be published irregularly, without a definite publishing date. The term *serial* connotes a large range of materials. Serials may include daily newspapers, popular magazines such as *Time, Newsweek, Good Housekeeping;* professional journals such as *Library Journal, Information Technology, American Historical Review;* proceedings of learned societies and conferences such as *Proceedings of the Annual Conference: Quality in Off-Campus Credit Programs;* or many reference materials that are usually considered books, but, technically speaking, because they are published continuously, are serials; *The World Almanac* and *Books of Facts* and *The Annual of Bookmaking* are good examples. Depending on the nature of the serial titles, they are commonly referred to as magazines (for popular reading), journals (publications devoted to a certain subject with in-depth coverage), or simply as periodicals, indicating that they are published periodically.

Besides serving as popular reading materials for recreational purposes, serials in professional subject areas contain the most up-to-date information on current research and discoveries in fields which are of substantial value to scholars, researchers, and students, and, therefore, are considered an important part of the library collection. Libraries usually have a large collection of serial titles and expend not only a large portion of their budget subscribing to serials but also considerable staff time in controlling and managing the serials area.

There are some unique problems in serials control. Library technicians working in this area must be familiar with the problems and must learn to deal with them. One problem is the change of a title and the numbering sequence. Sometimes the publisher will change the title of a serial completely or perhaps some of the words in the title. The serial may then carry continuous volume numbers or may start with new volume numbers. Sometimes a serial will become two different journals; sometimes two titles will merge to be one; sometimes one title will be absorbed by another. All of these changes can be very confusing for the library user unless exact information regarding the changes is recorded in the catalog. Another problem is lost issues. Normally, the serial titles are in complete sequence, yet very often issues will be missing, lost, or damaged and removed so that a gap appears. To get replacements for the needed issues is difficult and costly. Occasionally, the publication of a title is delayed, and sometimes the title ceases to be published altogether. Impeccable records are required on every title of the library's holding, from the first issue up to the moment; when the last issue arrived; when the next issue is scheduled to come; of all the changes that have happened to the title. Furthermore, claiming must be done for the missing issues; replacements must be ordered for the lost issues, and issues need to be prepared and sent to the bindery for binding; back issues need to be kept in order before they are sent to the bindery. Library technicians working with serials need to be knowledgeable about local policies and processing procedures and need to read the literature in the field to keep up with changes. Although the overall management of serials is not necessarily a problem, careful and systematic monitoring can become a labor-intensive, time-consuming, dynamic, and challenging job.

TERMINOLOGY

binding: In order to better organize the back issues of serials, and for the purpose of preservation, libraries regularly (once or twice a year) send back issues to commercial binderies so that they can be consolidated into one item. For example, one bound issue most likely will contain one serial's monthly publications for a whole year.

claiming: The process of informing the serials vendor or the publisher that a particular issue was not received and that a replacement copy should be sent to the library.

e-journal: Journals that are published electronically. The e-journal began with CD-ROM production; now they are mostly online and can be accessed through the World Wide Web, with or without paying a fee.

journal: A continuous publication consisting of articles in a specific subject field; also referred to as a professional journal. *Library Journal* and *American Historical Review* are examples. See also the definition of *serial*.

routing: When a new issue is received, it is forwarded to individuals who have expressed an interest in reading every issue of this title. When the first person is finished, the issue is routed to the second person on the list, etc.

serial: A title that is published consecutively in parts, and is intended to be published continuously for an indefinite period of time. It may have a regular publishing schedule such as weekly, monthly, annually, or it may be published irregularly, at a time deemed necessary and appropriate by the publisher. Serials are commonly referred to as magazines, journals, or periodicals.

serials control: Library tasks involved in managing serials titles and keeping them in good order and accessible to library users. Included are functions such as check-in, claiming, binding, replacement of back issues, and shelf maintenance.

USBE: An acronym for the United States Book Exchange, Inc. It is a clearinghouse for back issues of serials and old books. Libraries join as members and pay an annual fee, sending their surplus and duplicate issues to the USBE. When a back issue is needed, libraries pay a minimum fee to buy it from the USBE's huge inventory.

ORDERING

Bibliographic Verification

Similar to the acquisition of books or other types of library materials, when a serial title is to be acquired, complete bibliographic information must be in order. The necessary information includes the exact title of the serial, the frequency of publication, the price, the International Standard Serials Number (ISSN), and other pertinent information such as whether and where it is indexed. Depending on the individual library, the reference tools used to verify bibliographic information for serial titles vary. Two commonly used titles include *Ulrich's International Periodicals Directory* and *The Gale Directory of Publications and Broadcast Media.* More resources are found online, such as *MediaFinder* and *PubList.com.* Besides being used as verifying tools by the serials staff, they are good reference resources in general. Library technicians working with serials must also become familiar with the sources that are used locally.

Ulrich's International Periodicals Directory is published by R. R. Bowker in New York. It is a list of foreign and domestic serial titles arranged by subject fields. For each title, bibliographic and order information are included. It is kept current with an *Update* three times a year. Besides the print format, it is available in CD-ROM format and online.

The Gale Directory of Publications and Broadcast Media is an annual publication that provides information on newspapers, periodicals, and broadcasting stations in the United States.

MediaFinder is an online source for subscription to and information regarding print media and catalogs. It is organized by type of materials, in which magazines, newsletters, newspapers, and periodicals are all searchable categories. The Web site is <http://www.mediafinder.com/>.

PubList.com is a comprehensive directory of information about serial publications and newspapers around the world. Its Web site is <http://www.publist.com/>.

Periodical vendors usually supply catalogs listing the serial titles that they handle. Such catalogs are also used as verifying tools.

Vendors

If all their serial titles were ordered individually directly from their publishers, imagine the volume of work it would be to process the hundreds or thousands of individual invoices, renewing each title regularly, and generally dealing with countless publishers as different concerns arose. To facilitate the ordering, billing, and invoicing procedures, and to simplify the redundant tasks, most libraries use jobbers, also called dealers or subscription agencies, to order their entire list of serials or the majority of the titles. Some publishers, such as *The Reader's Digest* and *Ms.* magazine, for instance, will not allow a dealer to be the middleperson, and, consequently, libraries must subscribe to these titles directly from publishers.

Even though a serials vendor does not give a discount and does charge a service fee, it is still cost effective to employ this service. The vendor keeps the library's subscription list in order and sends an invoice once a year to the library. Besides keeping the subscription list, renewing the titles automatically for the library, and claiming missing issues, the vendor also tracks the problem titles, title changes, suspension, and cessation, all of which is of great assistance in time and effort to the serials staff in managing serial titles.

Some of the more prominent serials vendors are EBSCO (<http://www.ebsco.com/>), Blackwell's Online Bookshop (<http://www.blackwell.co.uk>), and Turner/Faxon (<http://www.faxon.com/>). Library technicians should be familiar with the vendor that is used locally, its services, and the procedures for conducting a close communication with its representative.

CATALOGING

The cataloging of serials follows the same principles as the cataloging of books, namely, using the *Anglo-American Cataloguing*

Rules, Second Edition, 1998 Revision, for descriptive cataloging, using the *Library of Congress Subject Headings* or *Sears List of Subject Headings* for assigning subject headings, and using the Dewey Decimal Classification or the Library of Congress Classification system to assign call numbers. However, the practice of a majority of libraries, especially small- or medium-sized libraries, is to eliminate call numbers for serial titles. Most libraries arrange serials on the shelves alphabetically by title.

Chapter 12 of the *Anglo-American Cataloguing Rules,* Second Edition, 1998 Revision, makes provisions for cataloging serials. The main difference from book cataloging is that the publication date, the starting date, or the first-known date is recorded with a dash and a space followed by the future closing date. If the serial has ceased publication, the closing date blank is filled in. The necessary bibliographic information also includes the publication frequency, the library's holding information, and, if there has been a title change, the previous title or the continued title.

Also in Chapter 12, what constitutes a title change is explained. If any word in the title other than an article, preposition, or conjunction is changed, added, or deleted, it is considered a title change. If the order of the first five words in the title is modified, a title change has occurred. Any title change requires that a new record be created.

On the MARC record, certain tags and fields are designated to explain serial characteristics. For instance, the tag 310 is used to indicate frequency, tag 780 is used for recording the preceding entry, and tag 785 is used for recording the succeeding entry. For a complete explanation of MARC tags and fields for serials, check MARC formats for bibliographic data on the Web site of the Library of Congress <http://lcweb.loc.gov/marc/>.

When using a bibliographic utility to perform copy cataloging, local holding information must be added. Figure 7.1 displays the bibliographic information of a serial title in MARC format, as required by a serials cataloger. When shown in the public display mode, the same record will display information as shown in Figure 7.2.

FIGURE 7.1. Sample Serial Record Display in MARC Format

```
001      854299
008      740411 19709999ilu                    eng    nam
020      0002-9769
090      Z 673 A5 B82
245 00 American libraries
260 01 [Chicago]|bAmerican Library Association
300      v.|bill., ports.|c28 cm
310      11 no. a year (July/Aug. combined)
362  0 v. 1-    Jan. 1970-
500      Official bulletin of the American Library Association
650  0 Library science|xPeriodicals
850      v.1(1972)-v.27(1996)-
```

FIGURE 7.2. Sample Serial Record Display in Online Public Catalog

Title	**American libraries**
Imprint	[Chicago] American Library Association
Location insert	South-Periodicals Z 673 A5 B82 Watch for
Identity	paper copy
Latest: *Received:*	April 1997 28:4
Descript	v. ill., ports. 28 cm
Frequency	11 no. a year (July/Aug. combined)
Pub date	v. 1- Jan. 1970-
Lib. has	v.1(1972)-v.27(1996)-
Note	Official bulletin of the American Library Association
Subject	Library science--Periodicals
ISBN	0002-9769

SERIALS CONTROL

Record keeping is most important for serials. The work is complete for books or videos, for example, once they are received, cataloged, and processed. Not so for serials; once a serial title is ordered, a record is established, and, from then on, the record needs to be updated as long as the subscription is active. There are steps

involved in keeping the serials records current. Every successive issue must be checked in, cataloged, and processed. When an issue
is not received, claiming must be done. When an issue is missing, a
replacement must be located. Then there are concerns such as
shelf maintenance and back-issue problems that need to be addressed.

Check-In

Each library has its own established routines for the check-in of
serials, which include daily newspapers, weekly magazines, monthly
journals, and other continuous publications that are published at
regular or irregular intervals. Check-in is the first step of serial
control. When a title is received, it is marked either on a check-in
card or on a computer. Different check-in cards are used for the
manual system, which include the weekly card, the monthly card,
and the daily card. The serial title, frequency of publication, bindery information, and any other needed bibliographic information
about the title is recorded on the card. When each issue arrives, the
proper box on the card is checked or dated. Figure 7.3 shows a
weekly check-in card bought from a library supply company.

There are many advantages to using the automated serial control system. Once the bibliographic information is entered into the
serial catalog, the record can easily be manipulated for updating
and other purposes, and an entry for the public catalog is also established at the same time. Furthermore, with the strike of a key,
other functions in serials control can be performed simultaneously.
The bibliographic records of all serial titles have been entered before the first issue arrives. When an issue is received, the library
technician will pull up the bibliographic record of the particular title and attach the volume number, issue number, and the publication date of the new issue. See Figure 7.4 for a serial check-in card
display on the computer screen.

Processing routines done at check-in include stamping the prop-
erty stamp, adding the security strip, attaching the bar-code label,
and any other tasks that are deemed necessary by the library, usually outlined in the serial check-in manual. For instance, some academic libraries copy the table of contents of certain journals and

FIGURE 7.3. Sample of a Check-In Card for Weekly Series

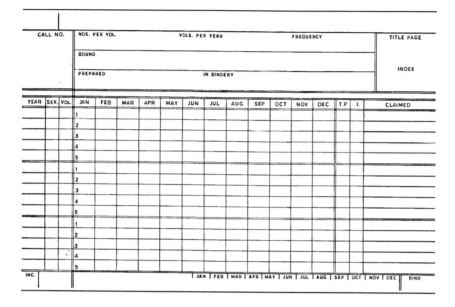

send them to interested faculty; some libraries produce a routing slip for particular titles and route the titles to interested staff members, etc.

Claiming

Claiming is an important process in serial management. When an issue is not received at the regular time, the claim should be made immediately; publishers usually do not print many extra issues, and the longer the time gap, the slimmer the chance of getting a replacement issue from the publisher. Claims can be made directly to the publisher or through a vendor, according to the agreement between the library and the vendor. Claims can be made on the claim form supplied by the vendor, in letter form, by telephone call, electronically via e-mail, or, if the library has an integrated system and it is connected to the vendor's database, through the serials control claim function. When claiming an issue, it is important to check the shelves first to make sure that the issue is actually missing. It is also

FIGURE 7.4. Serial Check-In Screen

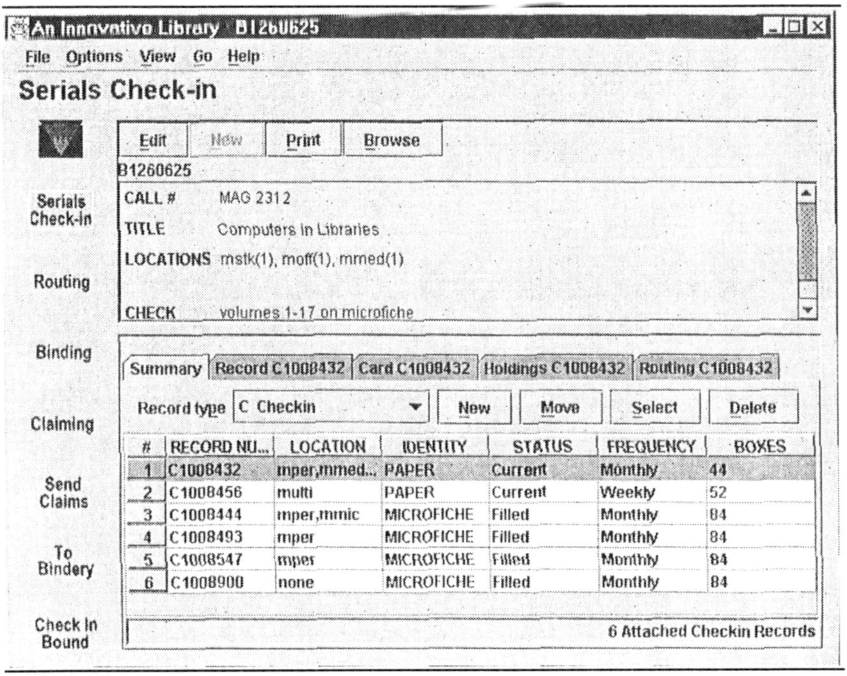

important to supply the vendor or the publisher with the specific item information for the issue such as volume number, date of issue, etc. Figure 7.5 shows a claim screen.

Binding

For preservation and safekeeping of back issues, serials are sent to binderies on a specific schedule so that titles can be bound annually/semiannyally or at some other frequency, depending on the library policy and the publication frequency. The library serials staff needs to prepare the following information, usually on a printed form, for the bindery: the exact title to appear on the spine; the exact position of the title; the color of the binding; the color of ink and the typeface, and other important information such as volume number and year. A library also needs to decide the frequency of

FIGURE 7.5. Sample Claim Screen

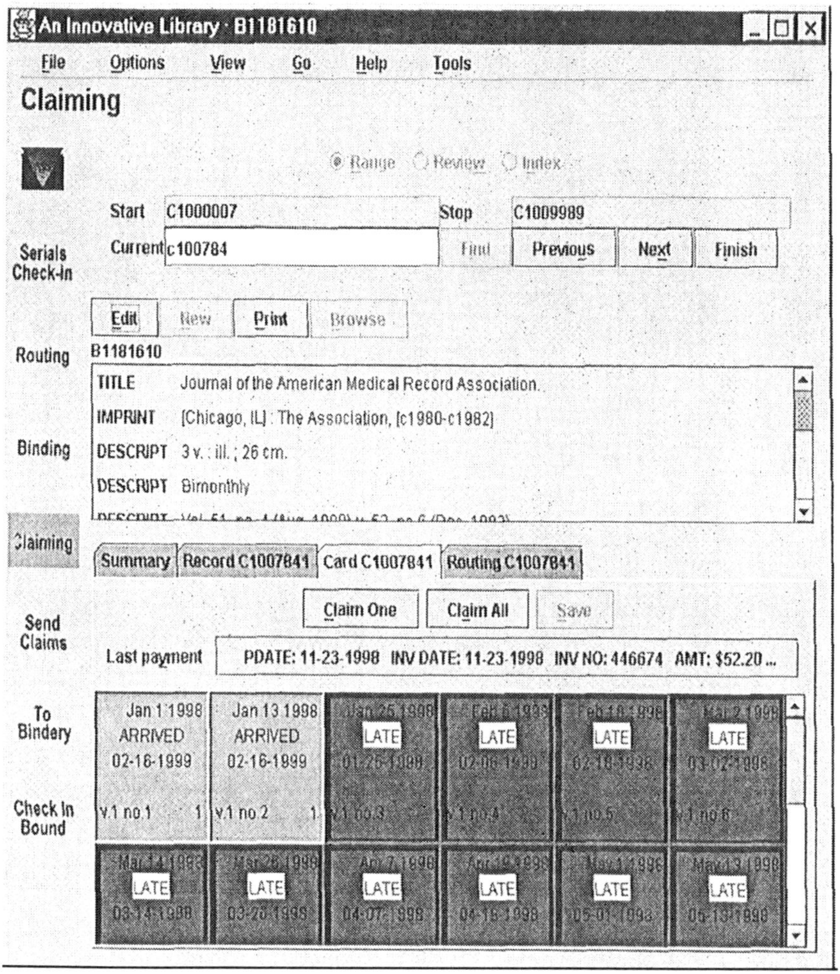

the bindings and maintain that schedule. Figure 7.6 shows a sample serial binding screen.

Not all libraries send back issues of serials to the binderies. Binding back issues is a time-consuming, expensive endeavor, and the bound issues occupy a huge amount of shelf space, which is at a premium in many libraries. It is standard policy for smaller li-

FIGURE 7.6. Sample Serial Binding Screen

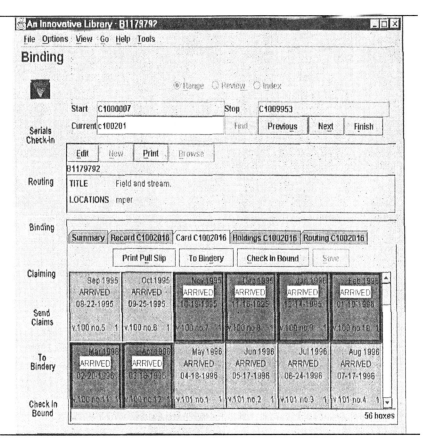

braries to buy back issues of serials in microfilm or microfiche format and discard the paper issues once the microform is received. Although some back issues can be found on CD-ROM and some online, it is hard to predict whether these media will be replacing the microform and the traditional bound form.

Replacing Back Issues

Occasionally a missing issue cannot be located, or an issue is found mutilated. In such cases, replacements must be ordered. As a rule, publishers do not print many extra issues, and therefore most often the publisher is not a good source for getting back issues. Some organizations and agents specialize in this kind of service. The United States Book Exchange, or USBE, is one such organization, as previously mentioned. It is a clearinghouse for all kinds of serials publications. Libraries join as members and send their unwanted surplus and duplicates to the USBE. When a library finds a need for a specific issue, an order is sent for seven dollars per issue, with the expectation that the serial is available from the USBE's inventory of 13,000 titles. For more information on the USBE and the titles that are available, check its Web site <www.usbe.org/>. Other commercial sources are also available. An Internet listserv called Backserv is a discussion group for serial staffs interested in back issues, duplicates, exchanges lists, and related topics. Library technicians working in the serials department can access this listserv and find more up-to-date information about back issues of serials.

Shelf Maintenance

Except for large universities and special libraries that keep their serial titles classified, libraries keep serials alphabetically by title on the shelves. Depending on the local policy of the individual library, only the most current issues may be on the display shelves, while back issues are housed in storage. Perhaps only more recent back issues remain on display shelves together with the most current ones. Shelf arrangement and maintenance should be convenient, current, and in clear order.

A serials holdings list, which includes titles and holding information, either in printed form or online, is essential for library users and is the responsibility of serials staff.

Libraries have special local policies and rules that dictate the length of time certain titles are to be kept. For example, some titles are kept for the most recent five years, while other titles may be kept for two or three years only. If the library purchases microfilm or microfiche for back issues, paper issues are discarded at certain intervals or as the microfom is received. The serials staff's duties encompass all responsibilities involved with keeping pertinent materials and discarding out-of-date materials according to the library's policies.

E-JOURNALS

In library serials management, more and more literature is being published about the management of e-journals. As many libraries have acquired e-journals—and many more libraries will acquire them in the near future—the management of e-journals has become an important consideration.

E-journal is the short form of electronic journal. These are the journals or serial titles that can be accessed from computer databases. Some are merely an online version of the print publication, and the library may purchase the print version or the print version together with the electronic version. Other titles are published electronically only, thus the traditional serials control model cannot be applied. E-journals started out in CD-ROM format and later, with the emergence of the World Wide Web, progressed to the online form, accessible through search engines designed for that purpose. The number of titles has increased dramatically; in 1999, there were about 5,000 e-journals on the Web, most of them scholarly publications.

E-journals have completely changed the scene in serials control. The role of the vendor has changed. The traditional vendor has become an aggregator. In the role of aggregator, vendors not only accept orders for electronic journals from libraries, they also provide proprietary search engines in order to assist the users, who can then retrieve the needed articles from the Web, wherever the article may reside. For example, OCLC offers an Electronic Collections Online service, which enables the user, with one search of the Web, to find information from a large collection of professional journals. Libraries subscribe to the journals directly from the publisher or a vendor but can gain total access remotely at OCLC. Another service is EBSCO online database, through which over 1,200 electronic journals are made available for subscribers.

Even though it is predicted that print journals will not disappear, at least not in the foreseeable future, it is nevertheless recognized that the number of electronic journals will steadily increase: the e-journal provides timeliness, ease of access, and a convenient format integration into a multimedia presentation.

The explosion of electronic serials has created an exciting development for library technicians responsible for serials control. Different ordering, cataloging, and processing procedures will have to be instituted to cope with the changes brought about by electronic journals. In the meantime, library technicians will be participating in all aspects of serials control, from knowledge of local policies and procedures in their own libraries to the big picture, which involves and coordinates computer and technology advances of the library world.

REVIEW QUESTIONS

1. What is a serial?
2. What variations in a serial title constitute a title change according to AACR2R rules?
3. Why is it important to keep an immaculate record for serials?
4. What is an e-journal? Will e-journals replace print journals because of the emergence of the World Wide Web?
5. How can a library obtain back issues of missing or lost journals?
6. Discuss some common problems in serial control.

Chapter 8

Preservation

A staggering volume of new information is continually being added to libraries. At the same time, old books crumble, old movie films become brittle, videotapes become fragile, computer disks deteriorate and data is wiped out, and new technology requires the abandonment of outdated hardware. Millions of books are deteriorating every day and, in fact, may be lost forever along with a large part of our civilization. Although acquisition of new materials is one goal every library strives to reach, preserving what is there should also be an important mission—one that is often forgotten.

TERMINOLOGY

book repair: Repairing damaged books in-house according to specific procedures and using appropriate supplies.

conservation: The act of physical and chemical treatment of library materials in order to retard their further deterioration; in other words, the technical activities of repairing and restoring damaged library materials.

deacidification: The process of treating books printed on acidic paper in order to make the books last for a longer period of time. Books are immersed in an alkaline solvent to remove the acid and to make the paper alkaline (or buffered).

digital library: A collection of digitized materials stored in computer databases. The originals may be books, articles, films, sound recordings, or any other medium. The images of the originals are scanned and converted to electronic data, and, together with a sophisticated indexing system, the materials become accessible to millions worldwide.

disaster preparedness: A plan that deals with prevention and damage reduction when disasters happen. The plan should include immediate response activities, recovery or salvage procedures, and treatment of damaged materials. It should also include information on where to go for further directions and assistance.

mass deacidification: A large number of books are usually put through the process of deacidification together; therefore, the process is referred to as mass deacidification.

micrographic technology: Technology used to reformat materials from paper-based originals to long-lasting microfilms. A state-of-the-art camera used for this purpose delivers high resolution, and the sophisticated optics and computer controlled exposures ensure a high-quality product. It is the preferred method for performing preservation microfilming.

preservation: The maintenance of books and other library materials to keep them as much as possible in their original condition. This is done by instituting preventive measures to slow deterioration as well as applying appropriate treatments to the materials themselves.

preservation microfilming: Materials are filmed to produce high quality 35mm microfilms, using micrographic technology. If stored in optimal condition, microfilm can last for about 500 years and therefore is considered the best reformatting medium for the preservation of library materials.

PRESERVATION AND CONSERVATION

What is targeted for preservation in a library? Because of the high cost of preservation and the potential destruction of priceless writings and irreplaceable resources, determining what is to be preserved involves important decisions.

The first factor to be considered is use. Policies and procedures should be in place to identify, during circulation and shelving, damaged or deteriorated materials. Because frequently used materials are obviously those that are necessary and popular with the library's users, they become the first target for preservation.

The value of the material is another factor in determining whether material should undergo conservation treatment. Because conservation treatment is more expensive than replacement, every effort should be made to preserve important contents through replacement first, even in a different format. A library should examine its own mission in relation to its preservation policy. For example, a research library is expected to preserve all of its material for historical and research purposes. It is also essential for a research library to preserve original copies for scholars and to show authenticity of a document. On the other hand, in a small- or medium-sized public library or a community college library, the main mission is to circulate current materials to its users, and under such circumstances, even though there are always some valuable materials that must be conserved, most worn-out or out-of-date materials can be discarded. In addition, the differences between a library's support for local needs or its role within a consortium versus its regional or national responsibilities should be recognized and considered in the preservation decision. Works that any library will keep permanently include local authors' works, local imprints, manuscripts, and archives.

THE PROBLEM OF DETERIORATION

The deterioration of a library's collection remains a problem as many elements contribute to the deterioration process.

Environmental Factors

What contributes to shortening the lives of library materials? What natural conditions put library materials in danger of physical deterioration? Natural enemies include heat, fire, moisture, light, pollutants, pests, insects, rodents, mold or mildew, and water. Steps that can be taken include temperature and humidity control; disaster preparedness; and protection against fire, water, dust, and dirt.

Harvard University, for example, has moved fragile materials out of the library and put them into a storage facility that provides an optimal preservation environment for its collection.

Chemical Factors

A large number of books printed from the beginning of the nineteenth century to the present are printed on acidic paper, which has a tendency to become brittle within fifty years. Recently, more books are printed on alkaline paper, which will reduce the pace of deterioration.

Air pollution is another factor that damages library materials. Particulate material can dirty and abrade paper, and common gaseous pollutants combine with atmospheric moisture to produce acids that corrupt paper.

Physical Factors

The human enemies of library materials include rough routine handling, improper shelving methods, food and drink contact that damages the materials, incorrect repair that shortens the life of the materials, using a book drop, and photocopying.

PRESERVATION EXPERTS AND ORGANIZATIONS

Library staff and archivists are charged with the responsibility of preserving materials and, when necessary, conserving them. Several professional organizations exist that are ready to offer consultation and assistance.

The Northeast Document Conservation Center in Andover, Massachusetts, was established as a nonprofit organization for the sole purpose of conserving paper and related materials. The Center offers the following:

1. *Conservation services:* Treatment of books and pages, restoration of original bindings, replacement of bindings too damaged to repair

2. *Microfilming services:* Microfilming of manuscripts, scrapbooks, brittle newspaper, and fragile books, including archival storage or master negatives
3. *Photographic copying services:* Duplicating historical photographs or preserving through microfilm, microfiche, or contact prints
4. *Field services:* Provide on-site review of collections, provide condition surveys, offer workshops on preservation and conservation, and offer emergency service through its disaster assistance program

Useful technical leaflets on all aspects of preservation works are also published by the Northeast Document Conservation Center and made available to libraries. One of its publications, the third edition of *Preservation of Library and Archival Materials: A Manual* can be accessed from its Web site at <http://www.nedcc.org>.

Preservation Resources is a division of the Online Computer Library Center (OCLC). It provides a full range of services to meet the preservation needs of libraries and other institutions. Services include consultation, workshops, microfilming, film duplication, polysulfiding treatment, digital scanning or microfilming, and indexing. For more information on Preservation Resources, check its Web site at <www.oclc.org/oclc/presres/about.htm>.

The American Library Association and state libraries, state museums, and state historical societies usually have in-house conservators or offer referral services that will guide libraries to find specialists who can be of assistance.

PREVENTIVE MEASURES

Environment Factors Control

Although experts disagree on the optimal temperature for book storage, it is safe to keep the temperature in library storage lower than 70° F. The suggested humidity range is 35 to 55 percent. Because fluctuation causes damage, the temperature and humidity should be kept constant. A minimal level of light, an air-condition-ing system, and an air-filtering system to prevent air pollution are environmental conditions that contribute to preservation.

Good Housekeeping Practices

Cleanliness and barring food from the library help eliminate problems such as cockroaches, rodents, and other pests. Library staff should be aware and monitor the collection periodically for mildew and mold, and apply proper treatment if it is discovered. A security system deters vandalism and theft.

Proper Physical Treatment

Proper treatment of books is easily accomplished and inexpensive yet too often overlooked. Many practices should become a habit of the library staff who handle the materials daily. The public must be educated about the hazards of mishandling library materials. Shelving books tightly causes damage to the spine upon removal from the shelf. Pulling a book from the shelf by using one finger to tilt the top of the book causes spine damage. Books that are kept straight or completely flat with a good bookend survive longer. An edge copying feature for library photocopying machines protects the spines of books. Air space at the back of book shelves, regular dusting, and attention to cleanliness with no food or drink allowed are simple but effective measures.

TREATMENTS FOR DAMAGED MATERIALS

Depending on the situation, the needs of the community, and the local policy of a library, decisions must be made regarding whether the damaged material is worth keeping, and, if so, what treatment should be applied.

1. *Discard.* If the content of the damaged material is no longer needed or is readily available under some other titles, discarding allows more space and eliminates redundancy.

2. *Book repair.* Improper repair may cause more damage to books in the long run. Library technicians must learn the proper methods of repairing library materials. For example, for mending

tears and damaged spines, proper treatment with Japanese paper and starch paste are required.

Supplies used for repair are available through commercial suppliers such as Archival Products <www.archival.com/>, University Products <www.universityproducts.com>, Brodart <www.brodart.com/>, and Gaylord Bros. <gaylord.com>. Some useful booklets are also available from these companies. For example, Brodart's *Simplified Book Repair*, Gaylord's *An Introduction to Book Repair* and *Simple Techniques for the Maintenance and Repair of Books* present step-by-step instructions with illustrations for book repairers to follow. *A Simple Book Repair Manual* contains information on book repair and is available from the Web site of the Dartmouth College Library at <www.dartmouth.edu/~preserve/tofc.html>.

3. *Binding*. For worn-out copies or books with loose spines, or to extend the lives of new paperbacks, books are bound either in-house or sent to a commercial bindery.

4. *Replacement*. If the worn-out or damaged material is commercially available, the most cost-effective means is to buy a replacement copy.

5. *Photocopying*. A single missing page, a mutilated page, or an entire book can be photocopied on alkaline paper and bound into book form.

6. *Preservation microfilming*. The intellectual content, if not the format of a brittle book, will be preserved if the item is microfilmed by taking a photographic image of the original and greatly reducing its size. Unlike regular microfilming, preservation microfilming is done only on silver-halide microfilm, allowing the film to remain readable virtually forever if the film is kept under optimal storage conditions. Preservation microfilming is considered the preferred method for reformatting unstable originals, such as brittle books, photographs, papers, and objects. It is inexpensive, easy to reproduce, and has a proven and verifiable standard for longevity. Materials are sent to preservation organizations, such as Northeast Document Conservation Center or OCLC's Preservation Resources, for microfilming, or their technicians will come to film the materials on site. The technology used for preservation microfilming is called micrographic technology.

7. *Optical disk reproduction.* Optical disk technology was considered an attractive medium for storage of information, primarily because of the disk's enormous storage capacity. It is an efficient medium as far as accessibility is concerned, however, data recorded on magnetic tape are prone to corruption and sometimes are totally erased. Furthermore, this technology is so new that its durability has not been proven.

Digital information becomes unreadable when hardware is updated or changed, and when operating procedures and software programs become obsolete. For preservation purposes, every time hardware is changed, all information needs to be copied and saved in the new format. With extensive amounts of information and data on the World Wide Web now, copying can become an unmanageable task. More on digitalization will be discussed in this chapter under the Digital Projects section.

8. *Mass deacidification.* Deacidification is a chemical treatment to stabilize acidic paper to prevent embrittlement and, ultimately, to prolong the life of a book. This is a preventive measure for which books are treated before they become brittle. The method impregnates books with magnesium oxide, which both neutralizes the acid in the paper and leaves an alkaline buffer behind, thus retarding the deterioration process. The deacidification process extends the durability of books for three to five times their original lives. When a large number of books are treated together, the process is called mass deacidification.

DIGITAL PROJECTS

Digital imaging and scanning technologies have been available for over twenty years. During that time, many digital library conversion projects have occurred. The process of converting digital images begins with the scanning of pages using sensitive scanning equipment, then the conversion of the information from pages to electronic data takes place, and, finally, storing the data in the computer completes the process. Yale University has launched Project Open Book, which has digitized 10,000 volumes on microfilm. The Library of Congress has a National Digital Library program where selected collections have been put into digital format accessible to readers worldwide. Digital images include those taken from original documents, books, microform images, and pictorial materials. They are available on the American Memory Web site at <http://memory.loc.gov/>.

Digital materials have many limitations. One is that the technologies are not standardized. The hardware and software must be compatible for one system to be able to communicate with another. Digital imaging technology is expensive and labor intensive. Besides the original costs, funding must be reserved for system upgrades, the addition of storage capacity, and data migration, which is transferring data from one storage medium to another when the technology advances. If migration is not possible when technological obsolescence happens, the data becomes inaccessible and therefore lost. Whether emulation, which enables different systems to communicate with each other, can be relied on for preservation is still unproven and cannot be used with confidence. Even if technology remains the same, digital materials are not expected to have a life span of over ten years. For materials published online only, such as e-journal articles, ironically, the preservation technique suggested by the experts is printing the material on acid-free paper. For more information on digital preservation, see the Council on Library and Information Resources' Web site at <www.clir.org/>. The last problem to consider is with the vast amount of information available on Internet Web sites. Absolutely no guarantee exists that the Web site that is there today will be there tomorrow. The problem of preservation of such materials and of optical media such as DVD and CD-ROM, which cannot be easily reformatated for preservation, is extremely complex.

For materials that will be preserved in their original format, a digital reproduction can be made to broaden accessibility, resulting in lessened use of the originals, which will protect the originals from being damaged and prolong their lives. Not a substitute or a replacement, but rather a surrogate, digital reproduction contributes to the preservation program, allowing for universal copying, distribution, and access.

DISASTER PREPAREDNESS

Disasters may happen at any time. Thousands of libraries have been damaged or destroyed by natural or man-made disasters. Disasters include flood, earthquake, fire, or leaky pipes. Some disasters may be avoided with proper planning and appropriate building maintenance. Even for unpreventable disasters, such as earthquakes or floods, libraries should have a disaster plan in place that articulates the library staff's responsibilities and what emergency steps must be followed.

A good disaster plan includes the following information:

- Prevention and protection strategies
- A list of telephone numbers for library administrators and emergency services
- A list of emergency supplies kept in the library
- A list of commercial companies to order supplies
- A library floor plan indicating all water and electrical connections and locations of fire alarms and fire extinguishers
- Procedures and priorities to follow in the event disaster strikes
- A list of people and organizations that can provide assistance and services

Several disaster plans planning guides are available on the World Wide Web. OCLC Preservation Resources <www.oclc.org/oclc/presves> and Conservation Online (CoOL) <palimpsest.stanford.edu> are good examples. These are useful resources that can be adapted when formulating a disaster plan for any library. The ALCTS section of the American Library Association Web site has also created a Disaster Preparedness Clearinghouse at <www.ala.org/alcts/publications/disaster.html>.

Water Damage

Water damage may result because of a flood, a pipe leak, or plumbing problem. For water-damaged books and other materials, according to the leaflet published by the Northeast Document

Conservation Center *Drying Wet Books and Records* (Technical Leaflet Handout 10 Emergency Management), five drying methods can be used. Following is a brief explanation of these methods. For more information, consult the leaflet and other reference materials.

1. *Air drying:* Air drying is best used for treating a few damp or slightly wet books and documents. The drying room must have temperature and humidity as low as possible. Fans should be used to keep the air moving. Single leaves of records can be laid out on tables, floors, and other flat surfaces, protected by paper towels or clean, unprinted newsprint. Coated paper must be separated. Interleave every few pages of books with paper towels or unprinted newsprint. Books should be completely dry before being returned to the shelves, and dried records should be put in clean folders and boxes.

2. *Dehumidification:* For damp or moderately wet books, this is the method that is most easily applied. Books and records are left in place, and large, powerful, commercial dehumidifiers are brought in. Together with controlled temperature and humidity, the dehumidifiers can dry the collection without the labor-intensive work of moving the collection or handling each individual volume.

3. *Freezer drying:* Materials are placed in a freezer as soon as possible after becoming wet. The very low temperature (below -10°F) will reduce distortion of the material and facilitate the drying process.

4. *Vacuum thermal drying:* Used for a collection that is water damaged extensively. Materials are put in a vacuum thermal drying chamber and dried as vacuuming and heating occur at the same time. Large amounts of materials can be dried at the same time, making it cost effective, but the result is less satisfying than other methods.

5. *Vacuum freeze drying:* Used for large numbers of very wet books, records, and coated papers. Although the cost is high, it yields the most satisfactory results. Wet books and records are frozen first, then put in a very sophisticated vacuum chamber to be vacuum-dried while still frozen. This method causes the least distortion of wet materials.

All methods of drying may be used successfully to different degrees of preservation, but that does not mean that materials can be restored to their original condition. In fact, once wet, books cannot be returned to original condition.

Fire Damage

A fire detection device and an automatic water sprinkler protection system are necessary parts of library building safety and maintenance. Regular inspections of the electric systems is also a must. A fire evacuation plan, which shows a clear and orderly evacuation route for both users and staff, is essential.

CONCLUSION

Preservation is an important yet often neglected component of technical services. Preservation awareness must be made a conspicuous element of everyday library operations and integrated into all library activities. Library technicians working in the preservation area should learn the skills of book repair and other specific techniques used for in-house conservation. For detailed instructions, several titles listed in the Suggested Readings section of this book are good resources. Some Web sites also provide useful information. A collection of information on conservation, covering a wide spectrum of topics of interest, can be found at <http://palimpsest.stanford.edu/>, titled *Conservation OnLine* (CoOL), which is a project of the Preservation Department at Stanford University. The Library of Congress has a FAQ (frequently asked questions) section on its Web site <http://www.loc.gov/faq/> dedicated to preserving library materials. Finally, Yale University Libraries Web site <www.library.yale.edu/preservation/progserv.htm> is a source of information on preservation as well.

REVIEW QUESTIONS

1. What is preservation?
2. What is conservation?
3. What causes the deterioration of books?

4. Briefly explain five treatment methods for damaged library materials.
5. What steps can a library take to slow the deterioration of library materials?
6. What is a digital library?
7. What components should be included in a disaster preparedness plan?

Chapter 9

Trends and Issues

TRENDS

For the past hundred years, libraries have evolved from being repositories of printed materials to providing all kinds of services involving materials of all types, including audiovisual materials, optical disks, such as DVD, CD-ROM, and online materials. The methods used for the management, organization, and distribution of information in libraries have changed also, and technical services departments have been the centers and the catalysts for those changes. Trends that are apparent can be summarized as follows.

1. Jobs performed in the technical services department have changed. Automation in the acquisitions and cataloging departments has streamlined operations, changing the nature of the jobs, making them more mechanical, refined, and precise and involving less decision making and judgment calls.

2. It is important for library staff to have computer skills as they are involved in working with a variety of systems on a daily basis and may be called upon to design and implement the online systems they use. Even job titles have included descriptive terms such as *technology, metadata, system,* etc.

3. The blurring of roles between librarians and library technicians has occurred. Automation and the use of bibliographic utilities have made it possible for most libraries to copy catalog, shifting the cataloging responsibilities from librarians doing original cataloging to library technicians doing copy cataloging.

4. Overlapping activities have occurred among library departments. Because the same database is used for all functions includ-

ing acquisitions, cataloging, and circulation, one department is usually assigned the task for maintaining the database, thus blurring the distinctions between library technical services and public services. Circulation, traditionally a public services function, is no longer only stamping or scanning books being borrowed by the public. It involves storage, maintenance, and retrieval of bibliographic data and increasingly is considered part of technical services. In the meantime, the acquisitions unit is broadening into collection development, and management has merged with the public services department, while the ordering function of the acquisitions department has been assumed by the cataloging staff.

5. More and more electronic resources will be collected by libraries. Cataloging rules will be modified to suit the electronic environment, or different rules, such as the Dublin Core, will be adopted universally for cataloging electronic materials. Library collections will include e-books, e-journals, and Internet resources.

6. The standard cataloger's workstation will be a PC equipped with all the necessary tools for easy access, such as the cataloging rules and bibliographic utilities. Internet resource links will be added to library's home page. Most tasks will be done on the Web.

7. Many libraries outsource at least part of the technical services operation, such as cataloging and processing or special projects such as foreign languages cataloging, to commercial companies or network services providers for more efficient and less costly services. Some libraries outsource all of technical services or even the whole library operation.

8. Networks and consortia, with shared cataloging, will provide Web access, and more libraries will join as members, thereby eliminating costly repetitive cataloging. Libraries will continue to be involved in other types of joint projects, such as cooperative storage and preservation activities, to cut cost and at the same time offer the best possible services to users.

ISSUES

With the advancement of technology and the emergence of the Web, the operation of libraries has changed tremendously in the past decade. Issues have evolved that will need to be addressed by the library field, including the following.

1. Dissatisfaction of library technicians is growing because of low pay and inferior status as their work becomes increasingly more demanding and professionally oriented. For library technicians, there is no established career ladder and no educational requirement; there is not even a uniform title. Yet library technicians are required to do the work of librarians in the technical services department.

2. There is a lack of educational programs to train future library technicians and to provide continuing educational opportunities for current library technicians. Because technology changes constantly, continuous training and enhancement of skills in the integrated system and in the use of computers, in a Windows or NT environment, are critical. Keeping up with changes in technology and information sources is the most challenging aspect of working in the technical services department.

3. No universal consensus has been reached on cataloging electronic materials. Should a library catalog only those items physically located in the library or all the items that library users have access to? Should rules in Dublin Core be followed?

4. In an online environment, accuracy and quality control become more important than ever. A small mistake may cause bibliographic records to be incorrect, inaccurate, misfiled, lost, or inaccessible.

5. Preservation of electronic data is an increasingly troubling issue. E-journals and Web sites may or may not be retained by their originators. Hardware upgrades often render data saved in older formats unreadable, and the long-term stability of the electronic medium has not been tested.

In the contemporary library environment, especially in the technical services area, library technicians have become an increasingly important component. With automation and networking, much in the traditional library operation has changed; however, the role of technical services remains the same as it always has been—that of developing, organizing, preserving, and distributing library materials for library users.

Suggested Readings

Association of Research Libraries. *Organization of Document Collections and Services*. SPEC Kit 227, Washington, DC: ARL, 1998.

Banks, Paul and Pilette, Roberta. *Preservation: Policy and Practice*. Chicago: ALA Editions, 2000.

Chen, Chou-sen Dora. *Serials Management: A Practical Guide*. Chicago: ALA Editions, 1995.

Christiansen, Christine, Ed. *New Serials Frontiers*. Binghamton, NY: The Haworth Press, Inc., 1997.

Cole, Jim and Williams, James W., Eds. *Serial Management in the Electronic Era: Papers in Honor of Peter Gellatly, Founding Editor of* The Serials Librarian. Binghamton, NY: The Haworth Press, Inc., 1996.

Conway, Paul. *Preservation in the Digital World*. Washington, DC: Commission on Preservation and Access. 1996.

De Pew, John N. *A Library, Media, and Preservation Handbook*. Santa Barbara, CA: ABC-Clio, 1991.

DeWitt, Donald L., Ed. *Going Digital: Strategies for Access, Preservation, and Conversion of Collections to a Digital Format*. Binghamton, NY: The Haworth Press, Inc., 1998.

Eaglen, Audrey. *Buying Books: A How-to-Do-It Manual for Librarians*, Second Edition. New York: Neal-Schuman, 2000.

Evans, G. Edward and Heft, Sandra M., *Introduction to Technical Services*, Sixth Edition. Englewood, CO: Libraries Unlimited, 1994.

Flood, Susan, Ed. *Guide to Managing Approval Plans*. Chicago: ALA Editions, 1998.

Fortson, Judith. *Disaster Planning and Recovery: A How-to-Do-It Manual for Librarians and Archivists*. New York: Neal-Schuman Publishers, 1992.

Fox, Beth Wheller. *Behind the Screens at the Dynamic Library: Simplifying Essential Operations*. Chicago: American Library Association, 1990.

Fritz, Deborah A. *Cataloging with AACR2R and USMARC: For Books, Computer Files, Serials, Sound Recordings, and Videorecordings*. Chicago: ALA Editions, 1998.

Gorman, G.E. *Collection Management for the 21st Century.* Wesport, CT: Greenwood Press, 1997.

Gorman, Michael. *Technical Service Today and Tomorrow,* Second Edition. Englewood, CO: Libraries Unlimited, 1998.

Greenfield, Jane. *Books: Their Care and Repair.* New York: H.W. Wilson, 1983.

Gwinn, Nancy E., Ed. *Preservation Microfilming: A Guide for Librarians and Archivists.* Chicago: ALA Editions, 1987.

Hamilton, Marsha J. *Guide to Preservation in Acquisition Processing.* Chicago: ALA Editions, 1993.

Hirshon, A. *Outsourcing Technical Services: A How-to-Do-It Manual for Librarians.* New York: Neal-Schuman, 1996.

Hunter, Gregory S. *Preserving Digital Information: A How-to-Do-It Manual.* New York: Neal-Schuman, 2000.

Intner, Shella S. *Interfaces: Relationships Between Library Technical and Public Services.* Englewood, CO: Libraries Unlimited, 1993.

Kahn, Miriam B. *Disaster Response and Planning for Libraries.* Chicago: ALA Editions, 1998.

Kao, Mary Liu. *Cataloging and Classification for Library Technicians.* Binghamton, NY: The Haworth Press, Inc., 1995.

Kao, Mary Liu. "Library Technicians: Education, the Workplace, and Job Satisfaction." Dissertation. University of Connecticut, 1998.

Lavender, Kenneth and Stockton, Scott. *Book Repair: A How-to-Do-It Manual for Librarians.* New York: Neal-Schuman, 1992.

McCombs, Gillian M., Ed. *Access Services: The Convergence of Reference and Technical Services.* Binghamton, NY: The Haworth Press, Inc., 1992.

Motylewski, Karen. *What an Institution Can Do to Survey Its Own Preservation Needs.* Andover, MA: Northeast Document Conservation Center, 1991.

Ogden, Sherelyn. *Preservation Planning: Guidelines for Writing a Long Range Plan.* Northeast Document Conservation Center, 1998.

Recognizing Six Finalists Who've Made a Difference: 2000 Paraprofessional of the Year Award. *Library Journal,* 125, p. 42, 1995.

Schechter, Abraham A. *Basic Book Repair Methods.* Englewood, CO: Libraries Unlimited, 1999.

Schmidt, Karen, Ed. *Understanding the Business of Library Acquisitions.* Chicago: ALA Editions, 1998.

Slote, Stanley J. *Weeding Library Collections: Library Weeding Methods,* Fourth Edition. Englewood, CO: Libraries Unlimited, 1997.

Smith, Linda C. and Carter, Ruth C., Eds. *Technical Services Management, 1965-1990.* Binghamton, NY: The Haworth Press, Inc., 1996.

Soete, G. *Preserving Digital Information.* Washington, DC: Association of Research Libraries, 1997.

Taylor, Arlene. *The Organization of Information.* Englewood, CO: Libraries Unlimited, 1999.

U.S. Department of Labor. *Occupational Outlook Handbook.* Washington, DC: GPO, 2000-2001.

We Are the Library. *Library Journal,* 120(18), pp. 30-35, 1995.

Wilson, Karen A. and Colver, Marylou, Eds. *Outsourcing Library Technical Services Operations: Practices in Academic, Public, and Special Libraries.* Chicago: ALA Editions, 1997.

Index

Page numbers followed by the letter "f" indicate figures.

AACR2R. *See Anglo-American Cataloguing Rules,* Second Edition, 1998 Revision
Acquisitions, 27
  and automation, 37, 38
  changes, 38
  files and records, 36-37
  preorder search, 28
  procedures, 32-35
  receiving, 34
  types of materials, 29
Air drying. *See* Drying methods
American Library Directory, 34
Anglo-American Cataloguing Rules, Second Edition, 1998 Revision, 43, 49, 50f, 64, 76
Application program. *See* Computer, application program
Approval plan, 27, 34
AsianLink, 22, 35
Associates: The Electronic Library Support Staff Journal, 7
Audiovisual materials, 30
Author number, 39, 53
Authority records, 20
Automation, 9. *See also* Technical services, and automation
Automation system marketplace, 25

Bibliographic information, 28
Bibliographic record, 39
  elements, 43, 44f, 45f
Bibliographic record notification. *See* OCLC (Online Computer Library Center)
Bibliographic utility, 20, 21-22, 47

Bibliographic verification, 28, 33
Billing records file, 37
Binding, 72, 93. *See also* Serials, binding
Blanket order plan, 28, 34
Book catalog, 42
Book number. See Author number
Book repair, 87, 92-93
Bookkeeping, 35
Books in Print, 35

C.A. Cutter Three-Figure Author Table, 53
Call number, 39, 54
Cancellation file, 37
Card catalog, 42
Catalog, 39, 42
  book. *See* Book catalog
  card. *See* Card catalog
  CD-ROM. *See* CD-ROM catalog
  COM. *See* COM catalog
  Functions, 42
  OPAC. *See* OPAC catalog
  types, 42
Cataloger's Desktop, 49
Cataloging, 40. *See also* Serials, cataloging
  copy cataloging. *See* Copy cataloging
  descriptive. *See* Descriptive cataloging
  importance of, 57
  original cataloging. *See* Original cataloging
  routines, 56
Cataloging in publication, 40, 46, 47f

CD-ROM (Compact Disc Read-Only Memory) catalog, 43
Chemical factors. *See* Deterioration, chemical factors
CIP. *See* Cataloging in publication
Claiming, 36, 73. *See also* Serials, claiming
Classification number, 40, 51, 54f. *See also* Dewey Decimal Classification System; Library of Congress Classification System
Client. *See* Computer, client
Collection development, 28, 31
COLT. *See* Council on Library/Media Technicians
COM (Computer Output Microform) catalog, 42
Computer
    application program, 9, 13
    client, 21
    operation system, 9, 12
    server, 21
Computers
    components, 11, 13f
    hardware, 11
    modem, 12
    monitor, 12
    software, 12
    types of, 10
Conservation, 87
Conservation services, 90
Consortia. *See* Networks
Consumer Information Catalog, 62
Cooperation. *See* Library cooperation
Copy cataloging, 40, 44
    bibliographic utilities. *See* Bibliographic utility
    cataloging in publication. *See* Cataloging in publication
    commercial sources, 46
    Library of Congress, 45
    print sources, 47
Correspondence file, 36
Council on Library/Media Technicians, 7
Criteria for Programs to Prepare Library/Media Technical Assistants, 7
Cutter number. *See* Author number

Cutter's Two-Figure Author Table, 53
Cutter-Sanborn Three-Figure Author Table, 53

Damaged materials, treatments for, 92-94, 96, 98
Databases. *See* Library databases
Deacidification, 87
Dehumidification. *See* Drying methods
Depository libraries
    designation of, 63, 64
    regional , 63
    selective, 63
    types of, 63
Depository Library Act of 1962, 63
Descriptive cataloging, 40, 48, 49
Deterioration
    chemical factors, 90
    environmental factors, 89
    physical factors, 90
Dewey Decimal Classification System, 40, 52
Dewey Decimal Classification and Relative Index, 41, 52
Dewey for Windows, 52
Digital imaging, 94
Digital library, 87
Digital projects, 94
    limitations, 95
    use of, 95
Digital scanning, 94
Disaster plan, 96
Disaster preparedness, 88, 96
Disaster Preparedness Clearinghouse, 96
Drying methods, 97
Drying Wet Books and Records, 97
Dublin Core, 41, 54, 102

E-journal, 73, 84
    ordering, 85
Electronic journal. *See* E-journal
Electronic materials, 30
Environmental factors. *See* Deterioration, environmental factors
Exchanges, 37

Federal depository libraries. *See*
 Depository libraries
Federal Depository Library Program,
 59-60
 purpose, 63
Fire damage, 98
Freezer drying. *See* Drying methods

*Gale Directory of Publications and
 Broadcast Media, The,* 74
Gifts, 37
Government documents. *See*
 Government publications
Government Information Locator
 Service, 61, 68
Government Printing Office, 60
 personnel, 61
 publications, 62
*Government Printing Office
 Electronic Information
 Access Enhancement Act of
 1993,* 61
Government publications, 60
 access to, 61
 definition, 59
 maintenance of, 68
 sales, 62
GPO. *See* Government Printing Office
GPO Classification Manual, 68
GPO Locator Service. *See* Government
 Information Locator Service

In-process file, 36
Integrated system, 9, 24, 25
Internet, 23
ISBN (International Standard Book
 Number), 28
SSN (International Standard Serials
 Number), 28

Journals, definition, 73

Library assistant. *See* Library
 technician
Library automation, 13, 19, 101. *See
 also* Automation
 goal, 15-16
 and technical services. *See*
 Technical services, and
 automation
 vendors, 25
Library cooperation, 16, 19, 24
Library databases, 25
*Library Education and Personnel
 Utilization,* 4
Library Mosaics, 7
Library of Congress, 45
*Library of Congress Classification
 Schedules,* 41, 52
Library of Congress Classification
 System, 41, 52
Library of Congress Subject Headings,
 41, 50
Library organization, 2, 2f
Library personnel, 5f
 classification, 4
 qualifications, 4
Library processing routines. *See*
 Processing routines
Library public services. *See* Public
 services
Library support staff. *See* Library
 technician
Library support staff listserv, 7
Library technical assistant. *See* Library
 technician
Library technical services. *See*
 Technical services
Library technician, 1, 4
 importance of, 103
 professional organizations, 6
 responsibilities, 5
 in technical services, 8
 training programs, 6
LIBSUP_L. *See* Library support staff
 listserv

Machine readable cataloging. *See*
 MARC record
Mainframe computers, 10

MARC record, 19, 55f
  delimiter, 56
  fields, 55, 56
  format, 20, 45f
  indicators, 55, 56
  for serials, 76, 77f
  subfields, 55, 56
  tags, 55, 56
  tapes, 20, 46
Mass deacidification, 88, 94
MediaFinder, 74
Microcomputers, 11
Microforms, 30
Micrographic technology, 88, 93
Minicomputers, 10
*Monthly Catalog of United States
    Government Publications,* 62,
    63, 68

National Digital Library, 94-95
National Union Catalog, 45
Networks, 20, 24, 47, 102
Northeast Document Conservation
    Center services, 90-91
Notation, 41

OCLC (Online Computer Library
    Center) services, 22
OCLC Online Union Catalog, 35
OCLC Preservation Resources, 96
On-order file, 36
OPAC (Online Public Access
    Catalog), 43
Operating system. *See* Computer,
    operating system
Optical disk reproduction, 94
Order requests, 33
  file, 36
Ordering, 33
Original cataloging, 41, 48, 49f
  descriptive cataloging. *See*
    Descriptive cataloging
  subject cataloging. *See* Subject
    cataloging
Out-of-print materials, 31

Pamphlets, 29
Paraprofessionals. *See* Library
    technician
Personnel. *See* Library personnel
Physical factors. *See* Deterioration,
    physical factors
Preorder search. *See* Acquisitions,
    preorder search
Preservation, 87
  factors to consider, 88
  importance of, 98
  preventive measures, 91-92
Preservation microfilming, 88, 93
*Preservation of Library and Archival
    Materials: A Manual,* 91
Preservation resources, 90, 91
Preventive measures. *See* Preservation,
    preventive measures
Processing routines, 56
Producers, 32
Project Open Book, 94
PromptCat, 22
PromptSelect, 35
Public printer, 61
Public services, 1
Publishers, 32

Receiving. *See* Acquisitions, receiving
Regional depository libraries. *See*
    Depository libraries, regional
Research Libraries Group. *See* RLG
RetroCon, 22
Retrospective conversion, 20
RLG, 23
Routing. *See* Serials, routing

SAN (Standard Address Number), 34
Sears List of Subject Headings, 41, 51
Selective depository libraries. *See*
    Depository libraries, selective
Serials
  binding, 72, 80, 82f
  cataloging, 75-76
  check-in, 78, 80f
  check-in card, 79f
  claiming, 79, 81f
  control, 72, 73, 77, 83

Serials *(continued)*
 definition, 71, 73, 78
 holding list, 83
 importance of, 71
 ordering, 74
 problems, 72
 processing routing, 78
 replacement, 82-83
 routing, 73
 shelf maintenance, 83
 title change, 76
 vendors. *See* Vendors
Server. *See* Computer, server
Standing order, 28
 file, 36
 plan, 34
Subject cataloging, 41, 48, 50
Subject heading, 41, 51f
SuDoc Classification System. *See*
 Superintendent of Documents
 Classification System
Supercomputers, 10
Superintendent of Documents, 61
Superintendent of Documents
 Classification System, 60, 64,
 65
 elements, 66-67

Technical services, 1, 2-3, 3f
 and automation, 15
 changes, 15
 and computers, 15
 issues, 103
 and library technicians, 8

Technical services *(continued)*
 relation with public services, 3, 101
 trends, 101-102
TechPro, 22
Trends. *See* Technical services, trends
Turnkey system, 9, 14. *See also*
 Integrated system

Ulrich's International Periodicals
 Directory, 74
United States Book Exchange. *See*
 USBE
USBE, 73, 83

Vacuum freeze drying. *See* Drying
 methods
Vacuum thermal drying. *See* Drying
 methods
Vendors, 29, 75
 selection criteria, 32

Water damage, 96
WebOPAC, 43
Weeding, 29, 31
Work marks, 53
World Wide Web, 21, 23

Z39.50, 21, 23

Order Your Own Copy of
This Important Book for Your Personal Library!

INTRODUCTION TO TECHNICAL SERVICES FOR LIBRARY TECHNICIANS

_____ in hardbound at $34.95 (ISBN: 0-7890-1488-2)

_____ in softbound at $22.95 (ISBN: 0-7890-1489-0)

COST OF BOOKS_____

OUTSIDE USA/CANADA/
MEXICO: ADD 20%____

POSTAGE & HANDLING_____
*(US: $4.00 for first book & $1.50
for each additional book)
Outside US: $5.00 for first book
& $2.00 for each additional book)*

SUBTOTAL_____

in Canada: add 7% GST____

STATE TAX____
*(NY, OH & MIN residents, please
add appropriate local sales tax)*

FINAL TOTAL____
*(If paying in Canadian funds,
convert using the current
exchange rate, UNESCO
coupons welcome.)*

❏ **BILL ME LATER:** ($5 service charge will be added)
(Bill-me option is good on US/Canada/Mexico orders only;
not good to jobbers, wholesalers, or subscription agencies.)

❏ Check here if billing address is different from
shipping address and attach purchase order and
billing address information.

Signature_____

❏ **PAYMENT ENCLOSED: $_____**

❏ **PLEASE CHARGE TO MY CREDIT CARD.**

❏ Visa ❏ MasterCard ❏ AmEx ❏ Discover
❏ Diner's Club ❏ Eurocard ❏ JCB

Account # _____

Exp. Date_____

Signature_____

Prices in US dollars and subject to change without notice.

NAME_____

INSTITUTION_____

ADDRESS_____

CITY_____

STATE/ZIP_____

COUNTRY_____ COUNTY (NY residents only)_____

TEL_____ FAX_____

E-MAIL_____

May we use your e-mail address for confirmations and other types of information? ❏ Yes ❏ No
We appreciate receiving your e-mail address and fax number. Haworth would like to e-mail or fax special
discount offers to you, as a preferred customer. **We will never share, rent, or exchange your e-mail address
or fax number.** We regard such actions as an invasion of your privacy.

Order From Your Local Bookstore or Directly From
The Haworth Press, Inc.
10 Alice Street, Binghamton, New York 13904-1580 • USA
TELEPHONE: 1-800-HAWORTH (1-800-429-6784) / Outside US/Canada: (607) 722-5857
FAX: 1-800-895-0582 / Outside US/Canada: (607) 722-6362
E-mail: getinfo@haworthpressinc.com
PLEASE PHOTOCOPY THIS FORM FOR YOUR PERSONAL USE.
www.HaworthPress.com

BOF00